Blueprints for Living

Perspectives for Latter-day Saint Women

Edited by Maren M. Mouritsen

Foreword by President Spencer W. Kimball

Brigham Young University

ISBN 0-8425-1812-6

Brigham Young University Press, Provo, Utah 84602
Printed in the United States of America

Contents

Foreword

The very number and nature of the challenges in today's world give rise to the need to assure ourselves in The Church of Jesus Christ of Latter-day Saints that we are doing all we can to prepare our wonderful women to meet those challenges that they, and all of us, face. It is very appropriate, therefore, that a conference such as this one, involving so many outstanding Latter-day Saint women, be held.

Believing as we do in the special place of women, both in this life and in eternity, the Church welcomes every appropriate effort to help women reach their great possibilities. Our Father in Heaven has a perfect love which he bestows upon each of his spirit daughters and sons, for God is clearly no respecter of persons.

It is a great blessing to be a woman in the Church today, but with that blessing comes great responsibility. Meeting that responsibility will require service, study, prayer, and a humble seeking of the Spirit of the Lord to guide in the quest for wisdom and knowledge.

Excellence is something to be sought for and earned by each of us individually. Therefore, as daughters of God, as our sisters, and as our friends, please know of our encouragement in all your efforts to achieve excellence in your lives. Moreover, know that we encourage you to educate yourselves for eternity, as well as to meet present needs, realizing always that there is no happiness except in righteousness.

May God bless you, the sisters of the Church, as you continue your life's journey, and may he bless the results of this Conference to assist you in that journey!

Spencer W. Kimball
President, The Church of Jesus
Christ of Latter-day Saints

Preface

On January 31 and February 1–2, the Women's Office of the Associated Students of Brigham Young University sponsored the Fifth Annual Women's Conference, "Blueprints for Living." The conference program provides this summary of the intent and focus of the conference:

> Our purpose in planning Women's Conference has been to create this type of an environment by designing a program that would help women to understand some of the many avenues available to them for self-improvement. The theme of the conference as well as the ideas for workshops have been taken from President Spencer W. Kimball's two Women's Fireside addresses. In these two speeches he discusses many of the important responsibilities we face in preparing ourselves for the challenges of today.
>
> It is our desire that this conference serve as a catalyst whereby those in attendance may find new beginnings or . . . accelerate preparation of their individual "Blueprints for Living."

The *raison d'etre* for this collection is to provide some of the comments from the Conference to a larger audience than the more than 4,000 women who were in attendance. It can also serve as a beginning point for both men and women as they cultivate and enlarge upon their understanding of some of the principles that were considered at the Conference.

President Spencer W. Kimball, in keeping with his ongoing encouragement to women, has written the Foreword to this volume. He has also consented to the reprint of his talk, "Our Sisters in the Church," which was given in the priesthood session of the October 1979 General Conference of The Church of Jesus Christ of Latter-day Saints. His talk followed his address to the Women's Meeting, held in September 1979, at which he indicated that he would address similar pertinent remarks to the priesthood bearers of the Church.

Part One of this book, "The Exemplary Womanhood Awards," provides a brief biographical sketch of and a significant address given by each of the three recipients of the Brigham Young University "Exemplary Womanhood Award." Beginning in 1975, the "Exemplary Womanhood Award" was introduced, and this award is now given every other year. Since 1975 three outstanding women, Belle S. Spafford, Camilla E.

Kimball, and Florence S. Jacobsen, have received this distinction.

Part Two contains the keynote addresses presented at the Fifth Annual BYU Women's Conference, "Blueprints for Living."

Finally, Part Three contains the text of the panel presentation, "Mormon Women: A Response to the World," given in connection with the 1980 Women's Conference.

An effort of the kind represented in the pages that follow is not a singular effort. There are many without whom this Conference or this volume would not or could not have happened. Special appreciation is extended to all conference participants for contributing to the success of the Conference itself. Speakers who worked to meet difficult publication deadlines aided the effort greatly. The ASBYU Women's Office, headed by the Women's Vice President, Jill Harris, provided overall direction for the Conference. Kimberly Ford, Conference chairman, and her committee are to be commended for an outstanding and successful effort in bringing people together to consider such important issues. President Dallin H. Oaks, Dean David M. Sorenson, and other administrative personnel at BYU provide a constant atmosphere of support and sound direction for efforts of this kind. John Drayton and James Bell, of BYU Press, have been enthusiastic in their embracing of this volume and thoroughly professional at each juncture of its preparation.

Above all, gratitude is extended to our prophet, Spencer W. Kimball, for leading and speaking out on matters of such importance to women of the world at this time. His counsel provided both the theme and the direction for the 1979 Women's Conference "Blueprints for Living:"

> It is true of all of us that, as we progress spiritually, our sense of belonging, identity, and self-worth increases. Let us create a climate in which we encourage the sisters of the Church to have a program of personal improvement. It ought to be a practical and realistic program, which is determined personally and not imposed upon them. Yet it ought to cause them to reach for new levels of achievement. We are not asking for something spectacular but rather for the women of the Church to find real self-fulfillment through wise self-development in the pursuit of righteous and worthy endeavors. (*Ensign,* November 1978, p. 104.)

Maren M. Mouritsen

Our Sisters in the Church

President Spencer W. Kimball

This address was given in the Priesthood Session of the October 1979 General Conference of The Church of Jesus Christ of Latter-day Saints. Reprinted by permission.

This general priesthood meeting provides a wonderful opportunity to thank you, the men and young men of the Church, for all that you do to lead good lives and to build the kingdom of God on the earth. We are eternally grateful to you, and we take notice of the fact that God has placed you on the earth now in order that your talents and devotion can be utilized in this important period of human history and the history of the Church.

Three weeks ago tonight the women of the Church, both young and older, filled this great tabernacle and assembled in the same halls in which you are meeting tonight. Unable to attend the women's meeting personally, I watched the proceedings of that glorious event by special television in my hospital room. My heart was filled to overflowing for the special blessing of the wonderful sisters of The Church of Jesus Christ of Latter-day Saints—God's heavenly kingdom here upon the earth. My beloved eternal companion, Camilla, read to those lovely sisters my brief message.

In that message I said to the sisters: "As we approach the general conference with its priesthood session, we will be no less loving or direct with the brethren, for our counsel will be similar."

I now want to make good on that promise to the sisters as I speak to you brethren.

We have all been blessed with special women in our lives—women who have had a deep and lasting influence upon us. Their contribution has been and is most important to us and is something which will be of everlasting value to us.

Our wives, mothers, daughters, sisters, and friends are all the spirit children of our Heavenly Father. I hope we will always bear that in mind, my

1

brothers, in terms of how we treat women. The sisters in this dispensation include many of the most noble daughters of our Heavenly Father. Let us always remember that God is no respecter of persons, but he loves us all, men and women, boys and girls, with a perfect love.

As President Harold B. Lee frequently said, "The greatest Church work you will ever do is within the walls of your own home" (see *Strengthening the Home,* [pamphlet] Salt Lake City: The Church of Jesus Christ of Latter-day Saints, 1973, p. 7). Many of us have repeated that many times.

Much of this special Church work will be judged by the way in which we serve and lead, in a Christlike manner, the women of the Church who are in our homes. I say serve and lead because the headship of the man in the home is to be like the headship of Christ in the Church. Christ led by love, example, and selfless service. He sacrificed himself for us. So it must be if we are leader-servants and humble patriarchs in our homes.

We must be selfless and give service, be thoughtful and generous. Our dominion must be a righteous dominion, and our partnerships with our eternal companions, our wives, must be full partnerships.

You wonderful stake presidents and bishops and your counselors and all of you brethren—please be especially thoughtful of the sisters who are, through no fault of their own, not presently given the blessing of being sealed for all eternity to a worthy man, so they do not inadvertently feel left out as we rightfully focus on family life. Do not regard their presence in your midst as a burden but as a blessing.

Ever bear in mind our special responsibilities to the widows, those who are divorced, others who are husbandless, and, in some cases, our young sisters who are fatherless. We simply cannot fulfill our responsibilities as men of God if we neglect the women of God.

Sometimes we hear disturbing reports about how sisters are treated. Perhaps when this happens, it is a result of insensitivity and thoughtlessness, but it should not be, brethren. The women of this Church have work to do which, though different, is equally as important as the work that we do. Their work is, in fact, the same basic work that we are asked to do—even though our roles and assignments differ.

It is because we prize our women so greatly that we do not wish to have them drawn away into worldly paths. Most of them are strong and good and true, and they will be the more so when they are treated with love and respect and when their thoughts and feelings are valued and understood.

Our sisters do not wish to be indulged or to be treated condescendingly; they desire to be respected and revered as our sisters and our equals. I mention all these things, my brethren, not because the doctrines or the teachings of the Church regarding women are in any doubt, but because in some situations our behavior is of doubtful quality. These things are not mentioned because of any sense of alarm, but because of a general concern that our people in the kingdom will need to become even more different from the people of the world. We will be judged, as the Savior said on

2

several occasions, by whether or not we love one another and treat one another accordingly and by whether or not we are of one heart and one mind. We cannot be the Lord's if we are not one!

We shall all be judged and held accountable for how we carry out our various Church assignments, and our mortal stewardship will get no more searching scrutiny than with regard to the way we have served and loved our families and our sisters and brothers of the Church. President McKay wisely observed, "No other success can compensate for failure in the home" (in Conference Report, April 1964, p. 5).

We love you brethren, and we love the sisters. We have complete confidence in you. We rejoice in your faith and your devotion to the cause of the Master. May God bless you and your dear ones as you return to them.

I know that God lives, my brethren (it is a great joy to say that many, many times), that Christ, the Redeemer of the world, is our Lord, and that this is his Church, The Church of Jesus Christ of Latter-day Saints, with Christ at its head. I leave this testimony with you, with my affection and my blessings and my best wishes.

Part One

The Exemplary Womanhood Awards

Introduction

Beginning in 1975, the Associated Students of Brigham Young University have honored outstanding women of The Church of Jesus Christ of Latter-day Saints by bestowing the "Exemplary Womanhood Award." Given every other year, alternating with the "Exemplary Manhood Award," this award has been presented to Belle S. Spafford, Camilla E. Kimball, and Florence S. Jacobsen and traditionally has been presented in connection with the BYU Women's Conference held each year and sponsored by the Women's Office of the Associated Students.

Following are brief biographical sketches of and talks given by each of the recipients.

The American
Woman's Movement

Belle S. Spafford

Nearly forty years of service on the Relief Society General Board and in the General Presidency, over twenty-nine of these as president, summarize the dedication of Sister Belle S. Spafford. Her service has spanned the lives of six prophets as well as much unrest in the world and change in the Church.

In addition to her years of service with the Relief Society, Sister Spafford has been and continues to be active in civic affairs. She has served in many positions with the National Council of Women, including a term as president from 1968 to 1970.

Numerous honors have been bestowed upon her over the years. She is one of two Mormon women to receive an honorary doctorate and she is one of three to receive the University's "Exemplary Womanhood Award." Many other universities have honored her with similar awards and honorary degrees. Though in her eighties, she continues to have great influence both in civic and Church affairs. Her model of excellence and competence remains an inspiration to women of the Church and the world.

A charming, gracious woman, she has filled her life with productive, useful, loving service. She has reared an outstanding family and has devoted much of her life to helping other women find productive opportunities in living.

The following address was given in July 1974 at the Lochinvar Club in New York City.

It is always with certain misgivings, I believe, that one speaks to such a distinguished group as is here assembled. These feelings are compounded when it is known that there are differing viewpoints on the subject. This is the position in which I find myself this evening in speaking on "The American Woman's Movement." A further difficulty presents itself in highlighting significant events covering a two-hundred-year period.

The intensity of activity in recent years on the part of certain women's groups, as well as on the part of some individual women, in behalf of improving the status of women and removing what they regard as injustices, has been called by one editorial writer "the sensation of the hour."

The goals women's groups seek and the general interest of the public in what is happening are reflected in numerous newspaper and magazine articles, in bulletins, in radio and television programs, in editorials, in conference and seminar programs, and in other ways. For example, I assembled at random seventeen headlines from newspapers, magazines, and bulletins that were close at hand as I began preparation for this talk. To illustrate the nature of the articles, I cite a few headlines:

1. Report Shows Women Still Suffer Discrimination at National and International Levels in Education, Government, and Private Industry
2. Women Charge Discrimination in University Admission Policies and Scholarship Grants
3. Women Seek Ordination to the Ministry
4. Women Students Urged to Reach for Training in Traditionally Male Dominated Fields
5. Give Women Credit Where Credit Is Due
   (This referred to purchasing credit.)
6. Women Emerging as New Breed of Political Activists

One brave man published an article entitled "Women Filling Men's Jobs." The writer inquired, "What will this do to me and my ilk?"

Three major questions arise. First, are we in the midst of a new movement? Second, what has given rise to today's agitation? Third, what does it portend?

It is my opinion, based on some research and many years of identification with organized women, both nationally and internationally, that the current effort commonly referred to as "Woman's Lib" is an offshoot of what began in the early part of the nineteenth century. Traditionally, the activity has been referred to as "The Woman's Movement."

As times have changed and progress has been made in the lot of women, new demands have come to the fore, and agitation that they be met has been intensified in recent years.

To review the rise of the American woman since the 1830s, which is generally conceded to have had its faint beginnings at that time, is to see her taking part in one of the great dramas of the ages. It is to see a tremendous force, which had been partially dormant, brought into active exercise in the great work of the world. She moved onto the stage of this great drama when there was need for her intuition and intelligent service.

In colonial days women had more rights socially and politically than in the days of the early republic. In the matter of the franchise, colonial women usually had the right to vote. It is doubtful, however, whether they made much use of the privilege. A few women, however, as individuals, distinguished themselves in fields outside the home. The American Revolution produced women like Abigail Adams, whose letters and pamphlets, history tells us, "helped light the fires that blazed at Concord."

Following the Revolution, there was a dull interregnum in the life of the American woman. For almost half a century she seemed to have stood still. One historical writer declared that women were as silent as the tomb.

7

They probably were held less important in the social scheme than they had ever been before or were destined ever to be again.

In 1833 there began faint stirrings. A silent revolution was beginning to take form insofar as woman and her privileges and her work were concerned.

In the early part of the nineteenth century, Eli Whitney invented the cotton gin. It revived the slumping institution of slavery, which was growing increasingly distasteful to many women, who by nature were endowed with humanitarian impulses. Weaving came out of the home, taking with it numbers of women to work at the industrial power looms. The industrial revolution was being born. This and the distaste for slavery are generally regarded as being behind the stirrings of the women for greater freedom of action and better opportunities for education. Education for women at that time was confined, in the main, to the three Rs.

In 1833 an American institution of higher learning, Oberlin College of Ohio, under pressure we are told, opened its doors to women. It established a kind of annex, a female department, entitled "Collegiate Institute." The announcement had its pathos, its humor, and its general touch of patronage. The reason given for the action was:

> The elevation of the female character by bringing within the reach of the misguided and neglected sex the instruction privileges which had hitherto distinguished the leading sex from theirs. (Inez Haynes Irwin, *Angels and Amazons* [Doubleday and Doran Company, 1933], p. 39.)

Fifteen women enrolled.

In 1833 there appeared the first women's club to which one might apply the term in its modern meaning, "The Ladies Association for the Education of Females" of Jacksonville, Illinois. Then came "The Female Anti-Slavery Society." Both organizations were short lived.

An interesting story is recorded in a book titled *Angels and Amazons,* by Inez H. Irwin, in reference to a world anti-slavery conference held in London in 1840. The United States sent delegates, among them William Lloyd Garrison, who was expected to make the great speech of the occasion. Henry B. Stanton took with him his bride, Elizabeth Cady Stanton, and a few other women who were deputized as delegates, among them Lucretia Mott and Elizabeth Peace. When the American women tried to take their seats, the conference denied them recognition. After a long and agitated discussion, the house compromised by deciding that the women might not take part in the proceedings, but might sit behind a screen in the gallery and listen. William Lloyd Garrison, arriving late, acted with characteristic justice and generosity. He promptly took his seat with his country's women and insisted on listening with them. He did not make his speech. The event which perpetuates this conference in history, however, happened outside the hall and had nothing to do with black slavery. Hurt and righteously indignant, Lucretia Mott and Elizabeth Cady Stanton walked down

8

Great Queen Street that night, discussing the burning injustice of the day's proceedings. At home these two women had struggled against the handicap of having to keep silent. Now in England, which had already manumitted her black slaves, behind a screen they faced facts at last. They drew a logical conclusion that they should go back to America and begin agitation for women's rights. This was a highlight in the history of feminism. (Irwin, pp. 78–79.)

With the dawn of the 1840s there appears to have been a general awakening with regard to the power of organization and the need for it.

In 1842 a unique and significant event took place. A handful of women, members of a newly organized church, The Church of Jesus Christ of Latter-day Saints, residing in Nauvoo, Illinois (a western frontier town), approached the Prophet Joseph Smith, who presided over the Church. They appealed to him to organize them in order that they might more effectively serve the Church and the people generally. The response of the Prophet to the request was favorable. On March 17 of that year, The Female Relief Society of Nauvoo, now known as the Relief Society of The Church of Jesus Christ of Latter-day Saints, was organized according to parliamentary procedures. The major purposes of the organization were defined as education (with emphasis on religious education), the development of women, and benevolent service. (On the flyleaf of a biography titled *Life and Works of Susan B. Anthony,* vol. 1 [Indianapolis: The Bowen-Merrill Co., 1899], presented to the Relief Society, the author, Ida H. Harper, wrote this statement, "All honor to the Relief Society of The Church of Jesus Christ of Latter-day Saints, the first organized charity." It may be of interest to you that on the flyleaf of Volume 2 of the same work, presented to the Relief Society, the author in her own handwriting states, "To the women who were loyal and helpful to Miss Anthony to the end of her great work.")

Orderly procedures were marked out for maintaining and conducting the affairs of the Society. Under the direction of the presiding priesthood of the Church, the women were "authorized to direct, control, and govern the affairs of the society . . . in the sphere assigned to it." (Bruce R. McConkie, *Relief Society Magazine,* Mar. 1950, p. 150.)

Latter-day Saint women from the very beginning of the Church had held a position of dignity, trust, and responsibility. Their mental capacities were recognized, as was their right to develop their talents to the full: They had been given the religious vote almost with the founding of the Church in 1830. Elsewhere, this was at a time when few men and no women enjoyed this privilege. Now, these women had been given the unique recognition of having an organization of their own, a structure through which to advance themselves and give service.

At the third meeting of the Society, the Prophet Joseph Smith met with the women. In addressing them, he made this significant statement:

> I now turn the key in your behalf in the name of the Lord, and this
> Society shall rejoice, and knowledge and intelligence shall flow down

9

from this time henceforth; this is the beginning of better days to the poor and needy, who shall be made to rejoice and pour forth blessings on your heads. (Joseph Smith, *History of The Church of Jesus Christ of Latter-day Saints,* ed. B. H. Roberts, 7 vols. [Salt Lake City: The Church of Jesus Christ of Latter-day Saints, 1932–51], 4:607.)

I have already referred to the limited educational opportunities for women extant at that time. Insofar as the needy were concerned, there were few private agencies for the care of the dependent, and public provisions afforded but one type of treatment—custody only for the poor, the feeble-minded, the insane, and the miscreant. Almshouse care was considered to be the most satisfactory method of providing for the poor. (See *A Centenary of Relief Society* [Salt Lake City: General Board of Relief Society, 1942], p. 39.)

As we consider our great systems of education today, as well as our vast private and public welfare systems, we must concede that this small group of organized women had listened that day to inspired words.

With reference to the words "turning the key" in behalf of women, *to turn a key* implies opening a door. Opening a door contemplates a structure built for some specific purpose, with doors through which people pass in using the structure for the purposes for which it was designed.

It is my conviction that the words "turning the key" for women implied opening doors of opportunity and advancement for them through the structure of an organization. It is my further conviction, shared by others, that the key was turned not alone for Relief Society women, but for women worldwide.

For those of us who believe in the overruling power of a Supreme Being in the affairs of mankind, it does not seem inconsistent to accept the words "I now turn the key" as divine afflatus in relation to women; nor in the light of future events does it seem unreasonable to regard this action as the actual beginning of organized effort for woman's emancipation from restraints that for years had encumbered her full development and usefulness.

Today the Relief Society, founded in 1842 with a membership of eighteen women, is national and international in scope. It operates in seventy countries of the world and has on its rolls the names of approximately 1.5 million women eighteen years of age and over, representing many nationalities. Its membership includes non-Latter-day Saint women as well as Latter-day Saint women, for the Society maintains an open-door membership policy. Its programs and instructional materials are now translated into sixteen different languages. Insofar as we are able to determine, the Relief Society is the oldest national women's organization to continuously persist.

And now as to what followed: In 1848, six years after the founding of the Relief Society, what is regarded as the first women's rights convention was held in the little Wesleyan church in Seneca Falls, New York. It was practically a small assembly of neighbors, but it threshed out the first Declaration of Independence For Women, demanding for them educational, industrial, social, and political rights. (Irwin, pp. 83–84.)

10

During the next forty years, organizations flourished in numbers. In 1888 the National Woman's Suffrage Association convened, in Washington, D.C., what is regarded by many women's organizations as the greatest women's convention ever held. It was called, so they announced, to observe the fortieth anniversary of the first public declaration of women's rights. The underlying purpose, however, was to further the cause of woman's suffrage.

Invitations to this convention were issued to seventy-seven women's organizations, selected as being either national in scope or of national value. Of this number, fifty-three accepted, among them the Relief Society. (It may be of interest to you to know that Utah women had been granted suffrage in 1870 and were conspicuous figures in the national woman's suffrage movement.) In addition to the delegates from the United States, there were in attendance representatives from England, France, Norway, Denmark, India, Finland, and Canada. Eighty speakers addressed the convention, but the central figure proved to be Susan B. Anthony. One of her biographers said of her, "In her black dress and pretty red silk shawl, with her gray-brown hair smoothly combed over a regal head, [she was] worthy of any statesman." (Ida Husted Harper, *Life and Work of Susan B. Anthony*, vol. 2 [Indianapolis: The Bowen-Merrill Company, 1898], p. 638.)

In addressing the meeting preliminary to the convention, Susan B. Anthony, with all the earnestness of her strong nature and with her voice vibrating with emotion, set farsighted views with regard to the platform. Said Mrs. Anthony:

> ... We have now come to another turning-point and, if it is
> necessary, I will fight forty years more to make our platform free for
> the Christian to stand upon whether she be a Catholic and counts her
> beads, or a Protestant of the straitest orthodox creed. ... These are
> the principles I want you to maintain, that our platform may be kept
> as broad as the universe, that upon it may stand the representatives of
> all creeds and no creeds—Jew or Christian, Protestant or Catholic,
> Gentile or Mormon, pagan or atheist. (Harper, p. 631.)

The chief outcome of this convention was the formation of the National Council of Women of the United States to be made up of national women's organizations or organizations whose programs were of national import, and the formation of the International Council of Women to be made up of national councils of the respective nations. Both organizations are active and influential today.

Dedicating themselves to the cause of suffrage, these organized women swung into vigorous action. It was not until 1920, however, that the Nineteenth Amendment to the Constitution was adopted, granting to women of the United States the right to vote and to hold public office. (May I say at this point that there are fundamental differences, in my opinion, between suffrage and what is contemplated in the presently proposed "Equal Rights Amendment.")

Women, however, appear to have been somewhat slow to expand their role in society, even after having been granted the franchise and other opportunities which they had demanded in their own declaration of independence. This was due, I believe, to a recognition of their lack of adequate training and experience in public life.

We recall also that war had descended upon the world, World War I followed by World War II. The wars seemed to entice, if not force, women out of their homes and into the labor market. After World War II an interesting phenomenon occurred in the world of work. A good portion of the women who, as a patriotic duty during the war years, had taken jobs, many of which were traditionally uncommon to women, felt a new independence; they saw advantages in the paycheck, and many of them never went back to the home and the life of a full-time housewife.

The desire of women to remain in the labor market and upgrade their employment opportunities was soon accompanied by an intense desire for training and education to qualify them for better job opportunities and a wider variety of services. The effort to thus upgrade employment opportunities continues.

According to a study made by a staff of Columbia Broadcasting System researchers, today more than fifteen million women in the United States have at least some college training, more than twice as many as two decades ago.

Concomitant with this training, there exist more and better work opportunities. In addition, the prevailing attitude toward smaller families, the rapid technological improvements affecting housework, together with economic need influenced by inflation have pushed increasing numbers of married women into the work force.

With this there has developed new demands by women for greater recognition, a determination to stamp out job discrimination on the basis of their sex, agitation for increased opportunities in the top policy and decision-making levels of public life. As I assess it, recently we have been passing through a period of upheaval. Agitation began with a few sporadic efforts by poorly structured groups, somewhat militant in character and extreme in viewpoints, gaining momentum until it has now become a national effort, commonly referred to as the Woman's Liberation Movement. Presently there are a number of well-structured organizations with dedicated members and determined goals. Militancy has largely subsided; although, in my opinion some extremism remains.

Among the big issues that appear to stand out are the demand for full equality with men in opportunities and rights, the determination to wipe out the traditional obeisance to the concept of male supremacy, and the intent to completely eradicate everything that tends toward denying woman full identity as a person or toward placing her in a position where she may be regarded as a second-class citizen.

12

The efforts to achieve these goals are being accompanied, in some instances, by shifts in some of the traditional values of life. Certain sacred patterns of life that have proved rewarding to both men and women and socially stabilizing, such as marriage laws and covenants, are feeling the impact. Certain new philosophies with regard to the character of home and family life are being aired which run counter to the time-tested traditional values. While the number of liberal advocates appears to be limited, their views are proving controversial. I cite a few of these views as examples:

1. The advocacy of de facto marriage (i.e., actually existing without legal action).
2. The attempt to eliminate male domination in monogamous marriage. There are those who affirm that legally monogamous marriage is the most male-dominated institution of all, and is the only institution in which women are expected to work without receiving any stipulated wage, as well as without having fixed working hours.
3. The determination to "throttle" the overproduction of babies. One viewpoint declares, "It's not women's lib that is downgrading the motherhood role; it is the ever more visible fact of overpopulation, and a reduction in the occupation of motherhood is now mandatory."
4. The efforts to curb the existing excessive voluntary service by women. The position of the advocates of this is that the volunteer worker robs another woman, who needs paid employment, of a job opportunity.

Some pollsters find that women in large numbers prefer the job of wife and homemaker to that of the unmarried woman working and seeking fulfillment in man's competitive working world. They prefer the gratification of motherhood, the privileges of wifehood, the position generally accorded the woman in the home by family members, and the status conferred by society on the title *Mrs.*

Some activists have openly stated that one of their big problems is the indifference of the average married woman to their efforts to liberate her from her traditional status of housewife.

The home and family are not alone in feeling the impact of new views and current demands. They are also being felt by business, education, and other institutions, along with government, as these institutions endeavor wisely to adapt to new concepts and new demands.

Withal, there are some things for which women are agitating that merit support: for example, equal pay for equal work and nondiscrimination in hiring practices when a male and a female applicant are equally qualified.

Personally, I am not in accord with those who believe that current problems and needs of women may best be answered by adoption of a constitutional amendment on equal rights. I am of the opinion that major advantages embodied in the proposed amendment could be achieved through regular channels of state and federal legislative action without raising questionable results.

I believe further that by nature men and women differ physically, biologically, and emotionally, and that the greatest good to the individual and society results where these differences are respected in the divisions of labor in the home as well as in community life.

Working with women in many countries of the world convinces me that there is no task to which woman may put her hand so broad and inspiring, so filled with interest, so demanding of intelligence and capability, so rewarding, as that of wife, mother, and homemaker. I regard this role as taking precedence over all others for women. In a well-ordered home, husband and wife approach their responsibilities as a joint endeavor. Together they safeguard the sanctity of the home. Their personal relationship is characterized by respect and enduring love. They cherish their children. In child rearing, I believe, there is no substitute for a caring mother.

A woman should feel free, however, to go into the marketplace and into community services on a paid or volunteer basis if she so desires, when her home and family circumstances allow her to do so without impairment to her family life.

Women owe it to themselves to develop their full potential as women— to exercise their mental capacities, to enlarge upon their talents, and to increase their skills—in order that they may give to the world the best they have in a manner that will produce the most good, regardless of the paths their lives may take.

I deplore the far-out views that openly break with those practices and procedures whose tested values over generations of time have contributed to the decency, stability, well-being, and happiness of humankind. I accept the premise that moral right is that which is true, ethically good and proper, and in conformity with moral law. What was morally right based on truth must remain right regardless of changing times and circumstances. Truth—and right that is based on truth—are immutable. We cannot afford to allow national sensitivity to become dulled into a calm acceptance of degenerating values and their demoralizing effects on our nation and its people.

What of tomorrow? I ask.

May I submit a few opinions, not that I regard myself in the slightest degree as a seer, but merely from the point of view of trends as I observe them and as I draw upon the past as I have noted it.

Just as the pendulum swings to and fro under the combined action of gravity and momentum to regulate the movements of clockworks and machinery and usually with the first push strikes hard at the far left and far right, moving somewhat irregularly and then finds its level, thus assuring the proper functioning of the instrument—so I believe will the pendulum of the current woman's action program perform.

Furthermore, I believe that without doubt many of the repressions and injustices which are troubling women today will be resolved. Gratefully, this is already taking place. I cite such things as equal pay for equal work under similar circumstances, new legislation on such things as property rights and nondiscriminating credit laws. This portends a better day ahead for woman.

Borrowing words from Marvin Kalb [expressed in a televised news cast], "We have no valid evidence that today's headlines will be tomorrow's wisdom." Undoubtedly some of the things for which women are clamoring today will be in the discard tomorrow.

Tomorrow we undoubtedly will hear less of woman's rights and more of her responsibilities and achievements.

Legislation may make legal the total equality of the sexes, but it is my opinion that the different natures of man and woman will be the supreme law in dictating the divisions of labor to which each will be drawn in the work of the world.

It is my experience that life, the stern teacher and the great disciplinarian, is now forcing upon us a recognition of the importance of spiritual and moral values. I believe a new day will find us moving forward toward primal religious, spiritual, and moral values, with materialism taking a lesser position. Man cannot live by bread alone.

I am convinced that the home will stand as it has stood during past generations as the cornerstone of a good society and a happy citizenry. While old activity patterns within the home may be modified by the impact of change outside the home, the enduring values which cannot be measured in terms of their monetary worth, their power for good, the need of the human being for them (such values as peace, security, love, understanding) will not be sacrificed on the altar of new philosophies and new concepts. Countless men and women and even children who have tasted these fruits of home and family life will recognize new philosophies which create spoilage in them, and they will fend them off. It is in the home that the lasting values of life are best internalized in the individual. It is this which builds good citizens, and good citizens make good nations.

President Spencer W. Kimball of The Church of Jesus Christ of Latter-day Saints has expressed the belief that the future of the nation, its success and development, are based largely upon the strength of family life. I am confident there are tens of thousands of Americans, men and women, who share this belief.

Robert O'Brien, senior editor of *Reader's Digest,* had this to say in an address given in May 1974 at a conference of the American Mothers Committee, Inc., held in New York City:

> In our hearts, we all know that the home is the cornerstone of
> American democracy. . . . It's well that the nation recognize and
> remember it, and engrave it upon the tablets of her history.

Throughout the ages children have needed mothers with their love and understanding guidance, men have needed wives, and women have needed husbands to share in the concerns and responsibilities of life. They have

15

needed the happy, loving, and protective companionship of one another. It will ever be so.

There is an old saying, "Man must work while woman must wait." The waiting period for the wheels of progress to roll around in behalf of woman (a period during which woman herself has worked as well as waited) is now nearly over. We may now say to her, in the words of Solomon, the wise man of Israel, "Give her of the fruit of her hands; and let her own works praise her in the gates." (Proverbs 31:31.)

Keys for a
Woman's Progression

Camilla Eyring Kimball

With her eager mind and spirit, Camilla Eyring Kimball is a woman of constant learning. She has an insatiable desire for knowledge. She has commented that—

I am not just satisfied to accept things. I like to follow through and study things out. I learned early to put aside those gospel questions that I couldn't answer. I had a shelf of things I didn't understand, but as I've grown older and studied and prayed and thought about each problem, one by one, I've been able to better understand them.

The daughter of Edward C. Eyring and Caroline Romney, Sister Kimball attended higher school at Juarez Academy in Mexico and two years at Brigham Young Academy where she majored in home economics and received her teaching certificate. In the fall of 1917, she began teaching at Gila Academy in Arizona. It was there that she met and married Spencer W. Kimball. They are the parents of four children, twenty-eight grandchildren, and nineteen great-grandchildren. Her husband and children are an integral part of her life, and her church service is central. Sister Kimball's intellectual interests have involved her deeply with civic organizations, clubs, classes, and study groups. She has taken a class almost every year since she has been married. Her life-long commitment to excellence keeps her excited about life. She feels that fulfilling obligations is the most direct opportunity to grow and that a woman should be alive to opportunities, involved in public interest, committed to her family, and determined to grow from service in the Church. Life is so interesting that it worries her that she won't be able to get done all that she wants to. Camilla Eyring Kimball is truly a woman who is ever-widening every aspect of her life.

The following address was given 3 February 1977 at the Devotional Assembly held at Brigham Young University in her honor.

I first came to Provo sixty-five years ago, a frightened, bewildered refugee. My family had lived in Colonia Juárez, Mexico, and was forced to leave in 1912 when revolutionaries in the Mexican Civil War threatened the Mormon colonies in Chihuahua and Sonora. I was seventeen when we fled by train to El Paso, leaving practically everything behind. I recall how

17

one of the revolutionaries brazenly lifted a woman's purse from her arm with the barrel of his rifle as she boarded the train. It was a traumatic experience for all of us to leave our homes and start again in a new country. For a few days we were housed in stalls in a lumber yard in El Paso, Texas. The curious came to stare at us. Finally Father came out of Mexico on horseback, and we rented some rooms. My uncle, Carl Eyring, was in Provo attending BYU along with his sister. They wrote, inviting me to come live with them and to finish high school at BYU. This was most generous of them, for they were hard pressed for funds enough to keep the two of them in school.

The next two years at BYU left me with indelible memories. They were hard, poverty-ridden years, but a time of great personal growth. I learned and prepared myself for employment as a teacher of home economics in the Church academies. I came to love BYU and through the years I have watched with a thrill as this school has grown tremendously in size and in world-wide influence.

I read the school papers and envy you the many wonderful cultural and intellectual opportunities. I have thought that when my husband and I get to retirement age, perhaps we can come to Provo and be active participants in the wonderful programs available here. I hope each of you has some sense of what a great privilege it is to be part of this institution and that you make every day count in learning and in making lasting friendships.

I appreciate this invitation to be with you at the beginning of this conference and share some ideas of how women can best fulfill their calling in life.

The Lord expects men and women alike, first of all, to grow in spirituality—that is, to worship him; to gain understanding of the kind of being he is and wants us to become; to develop deep, abiding faith; and to live by divine principles of conduct. No other school in the whole world is so richly endowed with the resources to teach the whole truth—to teach the important, eternal verities as well as the worldly knowledge we need for vocation and for enjoyment of life. Of all we learn in life, the single most important knowledge we can attain is a firm testimony of the Lord Jesus Christ as our Savior and an understanding of the path he would have us follow.

Sometimes we are accused of being boastful in declaring that we belong to the only true Church. But we say it not in pride, but in gratitude, considering ourselves blessed to have been born members of the Church or to have had favorable opportunity to hear the gospel preached so that we would understand and accept it. We reject no truth or good to be found anywhere, but we are anxious to share that added truth which we have. All truth is a part of the gospel. Truth is things as they were, as they are, and as they will be. We are not so arrogant as to assert that the Church program is perfect, for it continues to add programs to meet the changing times, nor would we say that its members are perfect. We have a long way to go before we have become all that the Lord wants us to be. But we do say to all who will listen, "Here is more truth than can be found anywhere else in this world because God has established his Church to teach his children so much as is within their present capacity to learn," and we say to others, "Come and share with us!"

Many years ago, when we were vacationing in Long Beach, California, I went to the public library to look for books to read. As I browsed through the shelves, a strange woman came up beside me and with no preliminary introduction said to me in a demanding voice, "Are you saved?" Taken aback, I paused a second to consider. Then I answered, "Well, I'm working on it." With firm conviction, she admonished, "You'd better accept Christ now and be saved, or you may be too late!" I have thought about this encounter many times since, and my answer to the question would of necessity still be the same today: "I'm working on it." Of course, our salvation depends upon our acceptance of Christ, but also on our continual progress and our remaining faithful to the end. Salvation is a process, not an event.

A major part of that process is in service. King Benjamin said, "When ye are in the service of your fellow beings ye are only in the service of your God" (Mosiah 2:17).

What shall we serve? Our first obligation is to our families.

So far as we know, the Church organization may not be found in heaven, but families will be. God joined Adam and Eve in the holy bonds of marriage even before they were mortal and commanded them to cleave to one another. God has through all ages fostered the family, giving to men the sealing power so that families can be joined for eternity. The importance of our finding worthy companions and of temple marriage cannot be overestimated when we realize that our eternal destiny depends in part upon this sacred ordinance. Without it we cannot have fulness of joy. With it the future is boundless. There are some who, from no fault of their own, do not have that opportunity in this life, but no one worthy of these blessings will be denied them indefinitely. Life stretches beyond mortality, and those who live worthily will find fulfillment in the hereafter.

As husbands and wives, parents and children, our foremost duty and opportunity for service is to one another. President McKay has said that "no other success can compensate for failure in the home" (in Conference Report, April 1964, p. 5). We must take advantage of every effective means to strengthen home ties.

The family home evening program has long been a part of the Church plan. I remember well as a child the occasions in our family where we gathered together and each child, beginning with the youngest, had a part on the home evening program. These are happy memories. When my brothers and sisters get together even now, we often reminisce about those times, repeating with laughter the poems and songs we performed back in those days.

19

It was fun to hear my brother Henry sing in monotone,

> What can little bodies do?
> Like us little lispers,
> Full of life and mischief, too,
> And prone to noisy whispers.

And Joe's oft-repeated contribution as a little three year old was,

> Three little rabbits went out to run,
> Up hill and down hill,
> Oh, what fun!

The songs the family sang together are still our favorites. Some of them were folk songs brought from England by our great-grandmother. We still sing these with our grandchildren, and these are traditions that bind the family together.

In recent years more definite and concerted effort is being made to perfect the program. We have come to realize that Monday family home evening should be as regular and important a part of our life as attendance at sacrament meeting, that it is worth sacrifices to keep this time special for those close to us.

Many people outside the Church are recognizing and adopting the family home evening program as a tool to strengthen their families.

Recently my husband spoke at a convention of young business executives and their wives at Sun Valley, Idaho. None of them were members of the Church, but several of them came personally to express appreciation for our family home evening manual, which they were using with their families.

A first major effort by the Church to reach the world with this message, the recent nationwide television program on home evening, has had much greater response than anticipated. Thousands of requests for the home evening booklet have been received from all parts of the country. What a chance, by precept and example, to have important impact on the lives of our neighbors!

We are by no means the only ones to recognize the importance of the family. Dr. Earl Schaefer at the University of North Carolina has affirmed that "parents and the home environment are more critical to a child's educational success than schools and teachers are." Three years of research has produced "a tremendous amount of evidence that parents' involvement with the child has the greatest impact in achievement, in curiosity, persistence—even creativity." It has long been said that children whose parents have read aloud to them learned to read better and with greater enjoyment than children who did not have such experience. Also, that those coming from homes where books were read, ideas discussed, and art appreciated proved to be better students than those who missed these experiences.

I am sure most of us could bear testimony to the value of our home environment, where family ideals were inculcated in us which provide lasting guidelines for our lives.

Young people anticipating marriage and family should keep these findings firmly in mind. Mothers with small children cannot overestimate the importance of the mother's place in the home with her children. Whoever shares that time with the children will largely determine their character and shape their lives. What a challenge for women!

I still have a vivid memory of my mother sitting at the table after supper in the evening with the lighted coal-oil lamp and an open book before her. As she read aloud to us, she at the same time was knitting stockings for the family. The click of the knitting needles punctuated the stories she read. I learned to love books and to reject idleness from her example.

Good books were always an important part of our home life. I remember, though, one day when I was small, I came home from the library with the book *Camille* by Emile Zola, anticipating reading it because the title of the book was so much like my name. The minute Mama saw the book, she exclaimed, "Oh, no, dear, you don't want to read that book." She promptly returned it to the library. A good many years later I read it and then realized that she was quite right in thinking I was much too young for it the first time. I am grateful that she loved me enough to establish standards in our home. The existence of reasonable rules is almost as important as their content.

Rita Chapman of Dallas, Texas, is quoted in the *Church News* as follows:

> I am totally convinced that once a woman has borne a child, she owes that child herself more than anything else in the first five years of his life. . . .
> I fear that raising emotion-starved and love-starved children can produce calloused, robotized adults—people who follow the group in straight lines and do exactly what everyone else is doing, because someone has said it is time.
> I fear for the working mother who is deluded to believe that some kind, patient woman will tend to her child's emotional needs until she can take over, that someone else will see that her child discovers he is unique, until she can pick him up at the end of the day—when she is perhaps so tired that the best he can hope to hear is, 'It's time to go to bed.'
> I fear for the future of the child whose hunger for love and recognition must be satisfied in large groups. I beg mothers to wake up, to experience the precious dawning of their child's life with him. Evening comes quickly—but in the evening may be too late." (*Church News*, 14 August 1976.)

The impact of what parents do in the home extends beyond the home, to community and nation. Michael Novak, in *Harper's* magazine, said:

> Throughout history, nations have been able to survive a multiplicity of disasters—invasions, famines, earthquakes, epidemics, depressions, but they have never been able to survive the disintegration of the

family. The family is the seed bed of economic skills, money habits, attitude toward work, and the art of financial independence. It is a stronger agency of education than the school and stronger for religious training than the church. What strengthens the family strengthens the society; . . . if things go well with the family, life is worth living. When the family falters, life falls apart. (See Michael Novak, "Family Out of Favor," *Harper's,* vol. 252 (April 1976), pp. 37–40.)

We are in a period when the great propaganda machines are telling us that for a woman to choose a career in home and family is somehow demeaning and that self-respect demands she pursue a profession of law or medicine or business. But rather than directing both marriage partners away from the home, we need to encourage both to make the strengthening of the family their primary concern. There is challenge, accomplishment, and satisfaction enough for anyone in this greatest educational endeavor—the home.

In the rural society of my childhood, we often lived close enough to grandparents, uncles and aunts, brothers and sisters, and cousins to use their physical and psychic resources to supplement our own. When we needed help, they were there. But in our highly mobile society today, this extended family is rarely so available. And today fellow Church members often fill that function. The visiting teacher and home teacher programs can provide support of this kind. Every family in the Church has two pairs of teachers who, taken together, should visit that home at least two dozen times a year with a spiritual message and a constant reminder that others care for us. We are responsible for one another. I help you and you help me. These visiting programs offer some of the strongest evidence that we truly are willing to serve one another and that the Church is an extension of the family idea.

In the Church organization there are ample opportunities for both men and women. I have felt no deprivation in not holding the priesthood. I feel only gratitude that I can, with my husband and sons, receive all its blessings without my having to assume many of its responsibilities. I have had teaching and leadership positions enough to give me full range for my abilities. In my fifty years as a visiting teacher of the Relief Society, I have had some of my richest human and spiritual experiences. In times of sickness and sorrow, there are very specific needs. In other homes you may be the only contact an inactive family has with the Church. The hand of friendship and fellowship is often the means of reactivation of these families.

It is clear to me that from an eternal perspective it does not matter where we serve but only how faithfully we serve. To each of us who has a calling as a teacher of families in the Church, I say be faithful and supportive, fulfilling that responsibility to the best of your abilities. And to each of us who is in a family being taught, I say let us make our teachers welcome and allow them to serve us, for in so doing we both shall be blessed.

If we want to give effective service to our families and our neighbors, as we are commanded to do, we must develop ourselves to our full potential. We need to enlarge our intellect and perfect our character. We need to become more Christ-like.

The pursuit of knowledge, which is characteristic of a university, is not only permissible, it is part of the gospel plan for us. The revelation given through the Prophet Joseph Smith in Section 88 of the Doctrine and Covenants sets the scope of our study:

> Teach ye diligently and my grace shall attend you, that you may be instructed more perfectly in theory, in principle, in doctrine, in the law of the gospel, in all things that pertain unto the kingdom of God, that are expedient for you to understand;
>
> Of things both in heaven and in the earth, and under the earth; things which have been, things which are, things which must shortly come to pass; things which are at home, things which are abroad; the wars and the perplexities of the nations, and the judgments which are on the land; and a knowledge also of countries and of kingdoms—
>
> That ye may be prepared in all things when I shall send you again to magnify the calling whereunto I have called you, and the mission with which I have commissioned you.
>
> And as all have not faith, seek ye diligently and teach one another words of wisdom; yea, seek ye out of the best books words of wisdom; seek learning, even by study and also by faith. (D&C 88:78–80, 118.)

My feeling is that each of us has the potential for special accomplishment in some field. The opportunities for women to excel are greater today than ever before. We should all be resourceful and ambitious, expanding our interests. Forget self-pity and look for mountains to climb. Everyone has problems. The challenge is to cope with those problems and get our full measure of joy from life. These "words of wisdom" from books are a means to that end.

Here and now you are much engrossed in textbooks, which are often tedious but important to the task of preparing for a specific career. They are keys that open doors, windows that open on life.

Some of the delightful pleasures of life are in continuing education in our mature years and in the collecting and reading of fine books. Continue to pick up interesting information in history, current events, the arts. There are various areas which we may miss in the few years we are enrolled in college, and learning confined to four years is soon out of date.

Through the years I have found it stimulating to be enrolled in a college class or two each year. The stimulation of association with young people helps keep one alive. For some years in Arizona I worked in the city library which was sponsored by the Federated Women's Club. I helped in the selection of books and found this a challenge to keep up with current literature. I still belong to one or another of the book clubs which bring a variety of reading material into our home, and I do make a concerted effort to select worthwhile books.

And beyond books, learning means keeping the mind open to all kinds of experience. Travel when you have a chance. Travel with an open mind, an alert eye, and a wish to understand other people, other places. That fits us all the better for most of life's callings.

When our children were young, every summer we, with them, made a trip by car to visit the different areas of America, east, west, north, and south. This way we gained a greater appreciation for our great country.

Going to Rotary International conventions, especially to Mexico and Europe, broadened our outlook. We worked at touring, seeing countries and people in detail.

For the past thirty-three years it has been my privilege, with my husband, to visit the members of the Church in countries all around the world. This has been an opportunity to get close to the people, to feel their needs.

The first fundamental need of every person is the indispensability of love to every human being, the feeling of being of value to others.

Our interdependence with others is the most encompassing fact of human reality. We need each other.

Much unhappiness has been suffered by those people who have never recognized that it is as necessary to make themselves into whole and harmonious personalities as to keep themselves clean, healthy, and financially solvent. Wholeness of the mind and spirit is not a quality conferred by nature or by God. It is like health and knowledge. Man has the capacity to attain it, but to achieve it depends on our own efforts. It needs a long, deliberate effort of the mind and the emotions and even the body. During our earthly life the body gradually slows down, but the mind has the capacity to grow even more lively and active. The chief limitations confronting us are not age or sex or race or money. They are laziness, shortsightedness, and lack of self-esteem. Those who avoid learning or abandon it find that life becomes dry, but when the mind is alert, life is luxuriant.

No learner has ever run short of subjects to explore. You can live most rewardingly by attaining and preserving the joy of learning and serving, combined.

Let me say in summary, with all the other knowledge which enriches our lives, let us not forget to include the knowledge of the gospel of Jesus Christ. When we think how fervently earthly parents want their children to grow up in faithfulness, we can appreciate in some small measure the great desire our Heavenly Father has that his beloved children may find their way back to him. Living the gospel is not the easiest way of life, but it is the most rewarding way.

I am grateful for the understanding we have of our responsibility to become Godlike in character, to love our children and neighbors as he loves us. The family is important enough to call for our best efforts—no profession is more noble than homemaking. The fulness of respect from good men and from God comes to those who fit themselves to serve and then serve one another—and family first of all—with love.

Nephi wrote:

> Wherefore, ye must press forward with a steadfastness in Christ, having a perfect brightness of hope, and a love of God and of all men. Wherefore, if ye shall press forward, feasting upon the word of Christ, and endure to the end, behold, thus saith the Father: Ye shall have eternal life. (2 Nephi 31:20.)

This is the greatest gift God has to offer.

I am grateful for the example set by Christ and for his great atoning sacrifice. I know that he lives. My prayer for us all is that we may follow his admonition to seek divine perfection in our lives and endure faithful and joyful to the end of our lives so that we may worthily claim our reward in his kingdom.

Our Heritage

Florence S. Jacobsen

Florence S. Jacobsen has distinguished herself as an exemplary woman through her many years of dedicated service as a church and civic leader. Having earned her bachelor's degree in home economics at the University of Utah, Sister Jacobsen served for eleven years as general president of the Young Women's MIA Board of The Church of Jesus Christ of Latter-day Saints. During that period she developed and expanded the Church's cultural program, started the Young Artist's Festival, coestablished the Mormon Youth Symphony and Chorus, offered scholarships for outstanding literary excellence, and was influential in the production of presentations that lead to the restoration of the Promised Valley Playhouse.

Subsequent to her release as general president of the YWMIA, Sister Jacobsen was called, in 1973, as the director of the Arts and Sights Division of the Historical Department of the Church. In this capacity she has developed many innovative programs, which have included the cataloging of Church buildings, a joint art-restoration project with Brigham Young University, as well as the restoration of many important sites in Mormon history. Some of these sites are the Lion House, the Joseph Smith home in Palmyra, the Brigham Young Forest Farm House in Salt Lake City, the Brigham Young and Jacob Hamblin homes in St. George, and the Brigham Young and Wilford Woodruff homes in Nauvoo.

In civic leadership, Sister Jacobsen has served as a member of the National Council of Women since 1961. She has also served as the chairman of the Child and Family Council, financial committee member to the International Council of Women, and an International Women's Year delegate. Locally, Sister Jacobsen has served on the governor's Historic and Cultural Sites Review Committee, the LDS Hospital Deseret Foundation Board of Directors and BYU advisory committees for Family and Consumer Studies and Family Life.

The following are excerpts from her address given 29 January 1980 at the Devotional Assembly held at Brigham Young University in her honor.

To be chosen to receive the prestigious Exemplary Womanhood Award has caused me to evaluate, why me? I know better than anyone—except possibly the Lord, my husband, family, and daily associates—my faults, shortcomings, procrastinations, deficiencies, and inconsistencies.

Many years ago in the presence of my father-in-law, I criticized the appointment of a man to a high position whom I felt was a poor choice. I knew he had similar feelings regarding the appointment; yet he said something that taught me a great lesson. He said, "Well Florence, it isn't what a man has been in the past or what he is at this very moment; it is what he may become that is important." I assume in today's world this statement is equally true for women.

In receiving this honor, I am grateful there is a tomorrow in which I can work toward being deserving of this award. I am very humble and overwhelmed to have been so chosen.

The first news of this event reached me through my secretary who put a memo on my desk that read: "The last week in January is BYU's Women's Week. You have been chosen to receive the Exemplary Womanhood Award, and your award is to give a BYU devotional address."

To decide what subject would be most meaningful to you has been a difficult choice. I would like you to know the history of the women's movement and of inspiring experiences of Mormon women who have served as officers of the National Council of Women of the United States, as officers of the International Council of Women, involving seventy-three nations of the free world, and as delegates to international conferences. I wish I could relate the unique experience I recently shared with Sister Belle Spafford in Bogotá, Colombia as we helped organize the American Regional Council of Women comprised of the nations of North, South, and Central America.

These are exhilarating assignments, when we as women are able to influence worldwide issues affecting the home, the family, United Nations policy, and even international legislation.

So many choices remind me of a personal incident. Our youngest son had just returned from his mission to Japan and was getting ready to go out on a date. Two days before, two of his friends had tragically lost their lives in an accident caused by a drunken driver.

As he put on his coat to leave, I, motherlike, said, "Please drive carefully. You have a great responsibility for the safety of both of you." He looked at me for a moment, and with a twinkle in his eye, he walked over, put his arm around my shoulder, gave me a little squeeze and said, "Okay, Mom, if you're worried about my driving, we'll park." He gave me no choice.

I also really have no choice as to my topic, for most of all I want you to know of our Mormon cultural roots and heritage.

The early artistic achievements of the Church members are a visible testimony to the world of their faith and are another evidence that the gospel of Jesus Christ has been restored. Their meticulous reverence for detail and excellence in such things as architecture, handmade pine furniture and woodwork grained to resemble beautiful hardwood, handwoven carpets, silk, cotton, linen and woolen fabrics, coverlets, music, and art stemmed from their devotion to the gospel. Their works reached such a high degree of excellence that similar products of the machine age of the Twentieth Century are, by comparison, mediocre. They believed the words of Joseph Smith when he said, "If there is anything virtuous, lovely, or of good report or praiseworthy, we seek after these things" (Thirteenth Article of Faith); and they did just that—they sought for excellence in all things.

I love the little verse Sister Ruth May Fox penned in the the front of her *Treasures of Truth* book. She wrote:

> I dedicate this book to the past, the present and the future—
> To the past, because I came out of it;
> To the present, because I live in it;
> To the future, because my children shall inherit it.

And so it is with each of us. Our history and cultural heritage are like families—they are forever, passed on from generation to generation. Personal records, journals, letters, receipts, art, and artifacts or each generation are important historically—not only to the past and the present, but for the future. It usually has been and still is the women, the mothers, and grandmothers who revere and preserve our great historical and cultural heritage from generation to generation.

Before the Church was organized, Joseph Smith, instructed by messengers from God, had scribes keep daily records. And it was revealed on the day the Church was organized, "Behold there shall be a record kept among you" (D&C 21:1). And while those assigned kept very good records, it is from the personal letters and diaries of the women that we learn the details of the early Saints' culture and daily life.

Brigham Young spoke of bringing the best of the world's art, artifacts, literature, and furniture to Zion to preserve them for the edification of future generations. In an epistle to the Saints published in England in 1848, he said, "If the Saints will be diligent in these matters, we will soon have the best, the most useful and attractive museum on the earth." We do not have the museum yet, but I believe in prophecy.

In 1973 when I was called by the First Presidency as Church Curator, the position had not been filled since 1919 when Elder James E. Talmage, who was the curator of the Church museum, was released. Brother Talmage had as his secretary a young law student by the name of J. Reuben Clark, Jr.

In reviewing the work to be done, we discovered that in 1965 a young man had cataloged some of the Church's historical artifacts. His cataloging system was a mystery to us—so we phoned him in Colorado and asked him why some of the catalog numbers had a "G" prefix and some "H." He explained that the "G" preceding the catalog number meant it had been previously cataloged by Dr. Talmage and stood for the "good" work he had done, and "H" stood for the "Heck" of a mess it was now in. (He used another word but my husband told me I couldn't use it because I am supposed to be an exemplary woman.) The mess is amost cleaned up after seven years.

Most of us have in our possession treasures once used and owned by a dear relative no longer with us. Such items are important historically and are part of our family and church cultural heritage. For example, when my father passed away we found hundreds of missionary farewell programs dating from 1912 to the time they were discontinued. We found wedding invitations dating from 1902, and on each invitation was written what gift had been sent and stapled to it was either the thank-you note received or a notation, "No thank-you received."

We also found letters we had written to him as children, our old school report cards, and personal letters; in fact, my father's whole life was there before us.

When my mother passed away at ninety-four, among her papers were sixty-one years of handwritten personal letters from her father, President Heber J. Grant, that we had never seen. Each one was a treasure.

As many have done before us, the family gave all of mother and father's letters, historical books, and documents to the Church Archives. It was impossible to divide these treasures among seven living children without destroying the collection. Now each of us has a copy of the letters and documents, and the Church has the original items.

I make a plea to all of you to write your personal history as our ancestors did and to preserve and treasure family art and artifacts of the past and the present. Someday place them where they can be protected, preserved, and displayed for the education of future generations.

When Brigham Young's words regarding a great museum are fulfilled, then the historical treasures of each generation will be on display to testify to Mormons and non-Mormons alike that the gospel of Jesus Christ has been restored and embraces all that is virtuous, lovely, of good report, or praiseworthy; and many, upon seeing the excellent work of families and the Church, will be inspired to seek after these things.

I am grateful for my personal heritage and for my parents who taught their children the gospel by example and by word. They left everything better than they found it by always striving for excellence.

They taught us that "There is a law, irrevocably decreed in heaven before the foundations of this world, upon which all blessings are predicated—and when we obtain any blessing from God, it is by obedience to that law upon which it is predicated" (D&C 130:20–21). In other words, there is no free lunch. You work for your blessings, and if you are not successful, you repent and start over, achieving one day at a time. They taught us, in addition to appreciation for our great cultural heritage, that we could not live off the heritage or the accomplishments of our ancestors and that we must be responsible for our own progress and success. Each day we should learn something new, and we should serve, love, and compassionately share all we have. These family teachings, our heritage, and the gospel in action become our responsibility to pass on to the next generation.

You are blessed to be able to build on the foundation of a great cultural heritage. But it is only through the gospel of Jesus Christ that we can achieve individual excellence and success as did our forefathers, who traveled the road before us.

The personal family heritage you develop and pass on can be the greatest the world has ever known—the heritage of the restored gospel of Jesus Christ. As uncertain as the world's situation appears, I want you to know that the Lord is in charge of this world. We each have the responsibility to carry out his commandments as individuals and as families and to set an unimpeachable example before the world so that all—seeing our reverence for our heritage and culture, and our kindness, thoughtfulness, forgiveness, our exellence, and love for all men—will want to become one with us.

This gift, the gospel in action, we have inherited, and it is our responsibility to pass it on until that day when the earth is prepared to receive again its director, our Lord, Jesus Christ.

Part Two

Keynote
Addresses

Blueprints for Living

Barbara B. Smith

Barbara B. Smith serves as general president of the 1.5 million-member Relief Society organization of The Church of Jesus Christ of Latter-day Saints. As such, she serves on numerous prestigious boards and committees, including the Board of Trustees of BYU. She also chairs the Childhood and Family Committee of the National Council of Women. Prior to her present calling, she served in various general, stake, and ward positions in the Church.

Mother of seven, and grandmother to twenty-three, Sister Smith is the wife of Douglas Hill Smith, the president of Beneficial Life Insurance Company.

This address was the keynote address of the Fifth Annual Women's Conference and was given 31 January 1980.

I am honored to participate this morning in the Fifth Annual Women's Conference planned and directed by the Associated Women Students of the Brigham Young University. After looking over the program, I feel a sense of well-being to know that you have so thoughtfully gathered together many outstanding Latter-day Saint women from whom to learn.

I want to take this opportunity to commend you on your selection of such a creative, accomplished, dedicated woman as Florence Smith Jacobsen to honor with the exemplary womanhood award. She is most deserving.

It is also a thrill to know that you listened to our prophet and then selected as your theme for this conference, "Blueprints for Living." I like that theme. It has the feeling of choosing, planning, constructing, of building a life by the conscious choice and the hard, self-determined discipline of well-directed efforts that are only possible through intelligent planning.

Recently I have been made very much aware of what goes into the development of a blueprint. My daughter and her husband have just decided to build a home. They are in the process of selecting and planning—blueprinting, if you will.

Let me review with you what I have observed in their exciting new venture.

First, they began by looking around for a lot, surveying all the available land in a location suitable for their needs. Then, when they finally found what to them was the perfect place for their house, they had it appraised and surveyed. Next, they purchased the property. Then came hours and hours of talking and intently planning together to identify the things they both wanted in their dream home. What style should it be: French, English Tudor, colonial, a ranch-type rambler? What general floor plan should they choose: one level or two? What kind of room requirements: a family room and dining room, and of course a kitchen and bedrooms, but how many, and where should they be located? And how many baths? With five children, a clothes chute into the laundry room was a must.

What extras could they afford within their budget? A spiral staircase, built-in, rotating storage shelves? A fireplace?

What special needs did each member of the family have? What are their needs, individually and collectively: a stereo cabinet for one child, full-length mirrors for another, study areas?

They began to consider how they wanted the house finished. Of what material should it be made: brick, wood, stone; or should they use some of the new and different sidings currently available?

What colors? Earth tones and pastels are good now.

And furnishings: period, modern, early American?

They spent hours putting down on paper their ideas, needs, and wants; then they sought the services of a good architect who could take their roughly sketched ideas, refine them, and then translate them into a blueprint. The blueprint is then to be professionally drawn with exact detail so it can be given to a builder who will be able to estimate the cost, materials, and the skilled craftsmen necessary to make that plan a reality.

Well, my children are just in the begining of this process, and I recognize that there are still so many fundamental and important decisions for them to make that it will be quite some time before they finally have a new home. But, as I thought about them and the years ahead, and reviewed the process of building, I was forcibly struck by the parallel between the process of building a home, which they are in, and the process of building a life, which you are in.

Let us focus our attention on four similarities:

1. Selecting our lot in life.
2. Building our life's foundation.
3. Constructing a framework for all we do.
4. Finishing the structure by becoming what we want some day to be.

That first step I mentioned, selecting the lot, surveying the land, and making related choices, begins early in life; and as you approach adulthood you have the responsibility of assuming the control and direction of your own life. In the decisions of adolescence we begin to look around us and form impressions of the world in which we live. Often we experience terrible growing pains as we have certain experiences. Some we choose, and others are thrust upon us by our parents, our peers, or circumstances.

Regardless of circumstances, you must ultimately decide what kind of a human being you are going to be, upon what philosophies you are going to build your life, and what style of life you will live. Will your choices be based upon worldly or spiritual values?

What attitudes toward the experiences or mortality will you develop? Do you favor the cool, noncommital way of breezing past events; or do you like a negative, pessimistic outlook; or, possibly, do you prefer a happy, optimistic attitude? I often think of a friend who smiled the moment she awoke. "I love to open my eyes to each new day," she confessed. There was optimism and enthusiasm in her approach—an attitude she *chose* to have.

What will you do with you life in your day-to-day living? How will you relate to the members of your family and your neighbors? Will you volunteer yourself to reach out to someone, or will you shut your eyes to everyone outside your own little circle?

What general scheme of planning will you adopt—a daily organized routine requiring self-discipline, or will you just let things come as they may?

Where will you stand in relationship to God? Will you have a program of daily prayer and meditation, will you become a scholar of the scriptures, or will you find yourself too busy to read? Will you choose to serve the Lord, or will you just wait and see what happens?

What kind of time are you willing to give; and what kind of planning for a lifetime of education, training, and continual growth do you want?

Experts who study human behavior point out to us that there is a great need for making a lifetime plan, realistically recognizing what each period of your life is likely to bring.

Alena H. Moris, president of Seattle's Individual Development Center, points out: "With some kind of a good design to life rather than a random existence which does not give security, one can lead a life that is potent and dynamic, one that provides all of the satisfaction of knowing that you are becoming what you are capable of being." (*Deseret News*, 10 April 1979.)

Childhood is a special time. It is one of enormous growth and development. I remember my mother once said, "Spend all the time you possibly can with your children; they will grow up so fast and leave your home that you will hardly know it is happening." I thought, "Mother, you've forgotten how long the time is when you are so hard at work with and for them." Now I know she was right. Like it or not, believe it or not, children do grow up all too quickly; and, in large measure, they reach out and participate in the excitement of learning only when it is encouraged and nurtured in their home and in the larger environment in which those early years are spent.

Can there be any wonder at the vital importance of the home when we realize the profound effect these early years have upon the lives of children? It is in the home that the life of a child is primarily shaped. The home is also the significant factor in determining the existence, or the nonexistence, of the basic problems in society such as divorce, crime, suicide, and all manner of social disorders.

After childhood comes the period of choice and preparation. That is where most of you are now, surveying the fields of interest, taking classes, and focusing attention on understanding and developing your personal interests and talents.

I hope you realize that your potential for study and the opportunity to develop new educational skills will probably never again be quite as available to you as they are now. In this springtime of your life you should concentrate on learning and preparing yourself with professional skills, with a single-mindedness that may never be possible again.

I believe that one never gets too much education. In fact, one great principle of the gospel teaches us that we need to commit ourselves to a lifetime of continuous learning, and I think that learning needs to include ways of applying in practical ways newly acquired information.

This period of your life is the time to upgrade your marketable skills, for no one knows when or where a woman might be called upon to provide the money to support herself. Elder Howard W. Hunter stated it insightfully when he said:

> There are impelling reasons for our sisters to plan toward
> employment also. We want them to obtain all the education and
> vocational training possible before marriage. If they become widowed
> or divorced and have to work, we want them to have dignified and
> rewarding employment. If a sister does not marry, she has every right
> to engage in a profession that allows her to magnify her talent and
> gifts. (Howard W. Hunter, "Prepare for Honorable Employment,"
> *Ensign,* November 1975, p. 124.)

Your surveying should include the selecting of a mate, one with whom you can share the world's experiences and one with whom you will be able to build an eternal companionship. This selection is the single most important decision one ever makes. Upon this choice depends your mortal and eternal relationships. It will determine how you care for the children you bear and how they will increase in stature, wisdom, and in favor with God and man. And it will determine your growth in these ways also.

Then looking way down the road, what happens when your children are grown and off in pursuit of their own interests? Where will you spend your time so that you can make the most of that season of your life?

All of this is but a part of that important process of selecting your lot. Land is not always what it seems to be on the surface. A careful builder always has a contour map made before his work actually begins. He needs to know what kind of underground water is present. Are there huge boulders under the surface? What is the composition of the soil?

You too should remember that in living your life you must consider the lay of the land. The Lord has counseled:

> Therefore whosoever heareth these sayings of mine, and doeth them, I will liken him unto a wise man, which built his house upon a rock:
> And the rain descended, and the floods came, and the winds blew and beat upon that house: and it fell not: for it was founded upon a rock.
> And every one that heareth these sayings of mine, and doeth them not, shall be likened unto a foolish man, which built his house upon the sand:
> And the rains descended, and the floods came, and the winds blew, and beat upon that house: and it fell: and great was the fall of it.
> (Matthew 7:24-27.)

No structure can long stand upon land that is faulty. Sandy soil will wash away, and no matter how strong the structure upon it, that building will be destroyed. So it is with you and me. If we choose to live in shaky, immoral environments, we have to recognize that the nature of the soil upon which we build will bring about our destruction.

After the lot is properly chosen and prepared, then the builder begins. He takes great care in preparing and pouring the foundation because he knows that a good, well-engineered foundation is critical.

Revelation from the Lord is the great foundation stone of all happy, productive living. He is the source of all truth and reliable knowledge. He has given you an open invitation to come to him for information, for direction, and for rest in times of trials and tribulations. A personal relationship to our God is essential for your firm foundation.

You need to know how the mortal and the immortal fit together. You need to know how heaven and earth interrelate. You need to know that you can communicate individually with your Heavenly Father.

How do you come to such truth? The blueprints that the Lord has provided—the holy scriptures—tell you to use profoundly practical steps if you wish to know. You might think of it in scientific terms: formulate a hypothesis, act upon that hypothesis, evaluate the results of the experiment, and then reevaluate the hypothesis in the light of the new information.

How could that work with the gospel? Well, you make an informed observation, your hypothesis. For instance: God lives. Then you begin to live according to that hypothesis. Study the scriptures, and read as Joseph Smith did:

> If any of you lack wisdom, let him ask of God, who giveth to all men liberally, and upbraideth not....
> But let him ask in faith, nothing wavering.
> (James 1:5-6.)

And the truth will be manifest unto you.

In Matthew 7:7 we read:

> Ask, and it shall be given you; seek, and ye shall find: knock, and it shall be opened unto you.

This invitation to the most profoundly important information in the world is repeated over and over again in the scriptures. In fact, in the new *Topical Guide to the Scriptures,* "Knock and it shall be opened unto you" is listed as appearing thirteen times in the Bible, the Book of Mormon and the Doctrine and Covenants. It seems to be a very important detail in the blueprint for living. It is repeated carefully, simply and completely, and often. Listen to the way the Savior expresses it in Revelation 3:20:

> Behold I stand at the door, and knock: if any man hear my voice, and open the door, I will come in to him, and will sup with him, and he with me.

The fundamental unity of Latter-day Saint women comes from the one thing that each of us can have: a testimony of an eternal plan of life and salvation; the testimony that God lives; the testimony that we are his children and that we individually have access to the powers of heaven; and a testimony that we are led by his prophet here upon the earth today.

The journals of the early Mormon women of this dispensation tell us that they were seeking light and truth, and they could not find satisfaction in their souls that what they had was enough. Then they heard about Joseph Smith, or they heard about the golden plates, or an elder came knocking at their doors and told them the truth had been restored. They asked the Lord if what they were hearing was true, and light came into their lives. The witness of the Holy Spirit was like a light being turned on in their souls. They would not and could not be persuaded otherwise.

Sister Eliza R. Snow says that her father, in assisting widows and others, was detained until the very last day of grace allotted to the Mormons for leaving the county; the weather was very cold, indeed, and the ground was covered with snow. She walked on to warm her aching feet until the teams would overtake her; meanwhile she met one of the so-called militia, who abruptly accosted her: "Well, I think this will cure you of your faith." The young heroine looked him steadily in the eye and replied: "It will take more than this to cure me of my faith." His countenance fell, and he responded, "I must confess you are a better soldier than I am." (*Eliza R. Snow, as seen through the Woman's Exponent 1872–87,* compiled and edited by Shirley Anderson Cazier.)

These sisters had a personal witness that the gospel was restored and that they could become part of building this Kingdom of God on earth, which would then take that glad message throughout the world. I suppose the poet captured the feelings of their quest and the personal nature of this foundation when he declared:

37

Back into the heart's small house I crept
and fell upon my knees and wept
and lo, He came to me.
(Author Unknown.)

If you remember nothing more of what I say today, I pray you will hear my own testimony and act upon this one truth. The strongest, firmest, most sure foundation for your life is a personal testimony of the truth that God lives, that he speaks again to us, and that he cares for each of us. This testimony will come to you if you will ask in faith, nothing wavering, and with sincere intent. My dear sisters, millions have a testimony, and it can be yours also if you will but ask the Lord in constant, secret prayer.

Third, any good house blueprint calls for a strong framework upon which to build. And so it is with life. The individual needs to construct a strong framework upon which to build. In building a house one selects good, firm timbers or strong, tempered steel that can bear the weight of the rest of the structure and withstand the ravages of weather and natural disaster.

In building a life, a person needs to choose good, strong tenets and assemble them into a design that gives stability and unity and yet allows for the constant addition of new information and further insights. This is the essence of gospel teaching.

The blueprint from the Lord suggests the need to build our lives using two fundamental principles.

The first is the personal quest for eternal perfection, achieved line upon line, precept upon precept, with each new insight giving us greater vision. When one seeks to be constantly improving, overcoming faults and weaknesses, and searching for enriching, enlarging opportunities, life becomes full of meaningful experiences.

Remember that perfection is a process, not a state we achieve. We are continually involved in learning today what will give us the information and experience we need for tomorrow.

The second fundamental principle is that we should give service to and perform acts of compassionate care for others throughout our lives, for doing so allows us to develop Godlike attributes.

Holding the framework securely together, and essential to every addition, is charity. According to the scriptures, without charity all else is as "sounding brass or a tinkling cymbal" (1 Corinthians 13:1).

Charity is the pure love of Christ—everlasting love—and except we have charity we cannot be saved. Further, we are shown in the Lord's blueprint that we should have charity for all, even those who despitefully use us, and that without charity all we do is of no value.

If we choose this sound, basic structure, we will have a life with endless potential. We will be able to spend our lifetime finishing the structure—completing it, furnishing it, and enriching it. That is why it is important to have a good blueprint. We should make our plans with such care that the structure will stand firm and unshakable. We can then imaginatively and creatively go forward with the finish work of our house.

We can prioritize the items we want to add until the structure iscomplete. In your day-to-day living, that means beginning to develop within yourselves the attributes that make you the kind of person you want to be.

You might begin by developing your talents. Each of you has special gifts, and the Lord expects you to develop them fully and then use them to help build his kingdom here on earth. You might begin by increasing your knowledge, or you might choose to begin by giving service.

When you begin may not be nearly so important as that you do begin. The gospel provides a vision of your fulfillment as a woman, an understanding of your future as an eternally oriented human being—a woman who is strong, competent, and filled with capabilities and commitment to a quest that will keep you constantly achieving.

I am sure you feel grateful, as I do, that you need not be fearful of life, for the Savior came to show the way and to conquer death. His atonement made possible your salvation and exaltation.

So if you are willing to accept the gospel blueprint and adapt the framework design to your own life, you can move forward, encouraged to finish your unique structure by developing all of your talents. You will look to the future with enthusiasm and hope, for the Lord has removed the pain of death and has taught that even errors are to be viewed as learning experiences.

Nothing that is for your good is forbidden, but cautionary signs do warn of those things that bring sorrow and unhappiness. Fundamentally, this mortal experience is to give you a variety of situations in which you can test yourself and develop the qualities that will make you worthy to return again and dwell with him who made us.

Perhaps even more basic is the realization that we should be developing the attitudes and character traits that will make us capable of eternal progression. Such is our birthright. The capabilities and powers are within us, and we must live to bring them forth.

When builders are working on a new structure, and the threat of bad weather comes or winter approaches, they quickly work to close things in. I've heard at least two reasons for this. First, good builders want to get the outer shell completed so that they can work throughout the storms to complete the inside of the building; and, second, they want to protect the interior from the ravages of bad weather because usually the materials that are needed in finishing the struture are not designed to withstand the elements in the same way as those on the outside. The finishing work needed to complete a life is somewhat the same.

I do not offer these suggestions as a matter of preferential priority, but I do suggest that both exterior and interior finish work are necessary. In fact, the finishing work in building a life is never completed. It goes on throughout mortality and throughout eternity. Change from the outside will occur just as surely as the sun rises and sets. Change from the inside will likewise occur—for the worse if we just drift, for the better if we determine to work to achieve goals.

Transferring our general ideas onto a blueprint and then transforming the drawings into reality requires many carefully detailed tasks and countless thoughtful decisions. It is the work of a lifetime.

In looking to the exterior finishing, let us be aware of the great variety of exteriors available. No two women look exactly alike. It was never the intent of the Lord that they should, but he enjoins us to know and understand the workings of our bodies and thereby to comprehend what helps and what hurts their functions.

A healthy body is more pleasing to look at and its movement more graceful, thus affording the benefits of both looking and feeling better. One of the Relief Society board members strives for a physically fit body by jogging in her room and memorizing scriptures at the same time— surely a pleasing combination.

The adornment of the human body is another point of exterior finish. It involves what you wear, your makeup, your jewelry, your grooming habits, your style preferences.

Brigham Young told the people there was reason to believe that the angels of heaven were lovely to look upon. He encouraged the sisters to be neat and clean and beautiful. He also felt strongly that fashion excesses were to be avoided. I think that kind of balance should still concern us.

We should all keep ourselves neat and clean. Most of us can do this. Some time spent in making ourselves attractive is important as it makes us feel better and helps other people feel better about us.

There is wisdom in developing one's sense of style. I once knew a young, attractive buyer in a large department store. She gave a talk to some blind women, at their request, about fashion and style. They had invited her to come to a meeting they held regularly for the purpose of helping them improve their looks.

She sat in that room as the preliminaries were being handled and looked at these well-dressed, sightless women. I don't know what thoughts went through her mind, for she was a woman trained in and sensitive to the visual line and color of ready-made dresses and coats.

But when she stood up and talked, she explained to them the one thing that was the most useful for them to know. I have thought about this many times since, and I believe it is the most useful single thing for any of us to know about clothes.

"Fashion," she said, "has to do with fad and style. That which is high fashion is often faddish in nature. It will be good for a short season, and then it will be gone. Style, on the other hand, is the fashion line which is classic in nature. It will always be in good taste, with perhaps minor alterations now and then."

So a person can be well dressed by paying close attention to the purchase of a dress with a style that will have a long life and by paying only casual attention to the faddish elements of the new season.

This same effort to develop good taste in makeup, hair styling, grooming of any kind, shoes, dresses, coats, jackets, and clothing of all kinds will make it possible for us to be attractive on the outside.

I think it is important to be mindful of the cautions given in the past that we not become slaves to appearance and that we not put undue emphasis on externals.

Nevertheless, how we look is important. Costume designers for dramatic productions spend their lives studying and trying to understand the language of external human appearances. And these appearances are very clever. They can create a mood; they can tell us something about a person's experiences in life; they can even tell us about a person's attitudes.

Sometimes on the stage, as in life, a costume will give you complete insight into a person's character and feeling. A very dramatic example of this occurs in the play *The Prime of Miss Jean Brodie*. Miss Brodie is a flamboyant teacher of young girls who has dedicated her life to molding and shaping the minds and characters of her charges. She is very romantic and a little unrealistic. The colors and the fabrics used for Miss Brodie's costumes visually portray these facets of her character in the scene where she comes into conflict with the headmistress. At the moment of dismissal from her position, she pulls on a grey coat; and as the top button is closed, the grey covers all the vibrant, romantic color, and we see the transformation of Miss Brodie. The color and the line of the coat subtly reinforce the pathos of the play.

It is very unrealistic to assume that the clothes we wear and the appearance we are satisfied with have no effect upon the course of our lives. They do. We all respond to the visual appearance of people and to our own appearance. We must make personal decisions about our exterior finish.

Another aspect of this exterior finish is the matter of manners—our social behavior patterns, our attitudes, and the effect they have upon our relationships with others.

Think about the endless detail found in the variety of patterns that our associations generate. We live in a world of constant change. The most constant thing of all is the continuing change in human relationships. The world of people is like a giant kaleidoscope. A twist, a turn, or even a bump, and the relationships of human beings to each other change and move; another forward or reverse turn and the relationships change again. It's a very exciting, worrisome, satisfying, puzzling, challenging world in which we live.

I would not like to leave you with the feeling that appearances and external relationships are so important as to justify spending all of your time with them. They are not, and you must use restraint and good judgment so that you do not waste precious time or become vain.

What I do want to point out is that your exterior finish does influence your life. It invites people to you and to some extent governs their attitudes toward you. It is also true that what we wear, how we look, and how we think about ourselves influence how we feel.

41

In the film *West Side Story,* Maria first discovers her feelings of love singing, "I Feel Pretty, Oh So Pretty." Of course it is proverbial that a woman in love looks beautiful.

A stage designer I know once conducted a workshop for the Church; and, as he was teaching the volunteers how to make costumes, some wanted to use a shortcut and hem the period skirts by machine. Painstakingly, he explained that the hand-stitched hems looked better because they would flow and move more easily. "That's important on the stage," he said, "because it helps the actress. If she feels that she looks graceful, she will perform better."

This is the reason I mention outward appearances and manners today. They are necessary to complete your life. The exterior finish of the house is what invites us in.

But of far greater significance is the finish on the inside. On the inside lies true beauty. On the inside lies the motivation for all that we do. You can select and polish those characteristics for which you wish to be known. Will you be honest? Will you be chaste? Will you be kind? Will you have integrity?

You and I alone determine the interior finish of our souls. The choices we make individually are the ones that ultimately set in place the furnishings.

Will you be part of the creative force that allows human life to continue on this earth? Only your personal decisions concerning the bearing of children, if you have a choice, can determine that. Will you be part of the rearing of children? Only your decisions and actions can determine that. Will you marry if a mutually satisfying opportunity comes your way? Only you can decide that.

Will you be lonely in this life? Probably. Everybody knows some loneliness. But will your loneliness engulf you and stop your progress? Only you can decide that. Single or married, you will have times of choice in your life. Will you seek out opportunities to give love or won't you? Only you can decide, but upon that decision so much else depends. One thing is certain, though: if you give love to all you encounter—and if you seek opportunities to give love to those who hunger and thirst and have great need—then love will flow back to you, and you will not be alone.

So it goes, down the whole catalog of human characteristics. Which ones do you wish to have? Which ones are you willing to cultivate and develop? The interior finish of your life depends upon such decisions.

One of the great teachings of the restored gospel is that each person has the right and the responsibility to determine the direction of his or her life. So it is with each of you. So it is with me.

The English writer, Somerset Maugham, who is known as a great cynic, once wrote a book called *Summing Up.* In this volume he describes each of the Christian virtues and puts them down one by one as being full of fraud or hypocrisy. Then he comes toward the end of the book, and he writes that, despite his disillusionment with these so-called virtues, when he finds himself in the presence of a truly good person his heart kneels in reverence.

So finish your structure with the characteristics of faith, hope, and charity, remembering that the greatest of these is charity. Seek wisdom and give service freely. In these ways you will adorn your life with the beauties that radiate from within.

Circumstances and opportunities will vary for each of you. You have to seek out those opportunities that will allow you to develop, and you must be responsible for the choices you make as well as the consequences of those choices for yourself, for others, and for society in general.

The Lord requires only that you do the best you can to gain experience and that you continue your growth by participating with a willing heart and teachable spirit.

Think often:

> The beauty of the house is order;
> The blessing of the house is contentment;
> The glory of the house is hospitality;
> The crown of the house is godliness.
> (Author Unknown.)

I testify that you will have order, contentment, hospitality, and godliness as you build your life according to an eternal blueprint.

Patriarchy and Matriarchy

Hugh W. Nibley

Dr. Hugh W. Nibley, currently a professor of history and religion at Brigham Young University and formerly director of the Institute of Ancient Studies, is certainly one of the foremost scholars in the Church.

Dr. Nibley graduated from UCLA in history with highest honors and received his Ph.D. from the University of California at Berkeley. Dr. Nibley taught history and languages at Claremont College. At BYU, he has been named Professor of the Year.

This address was given on 1 February 1980.

My story begins with Adam and Eve, the archetypal man and woman, in whom each of us is represented. From the most ancient times their thrilling confrontation has been dramatized in rites and ceremonies throughout the world, as part of a great creation-drama rehearsed at the new year to celebrate the establishment of divine authority on earth in the person of the king and his companion. There is a perfect unity between these two mortals. They are "one flesh." The word *rib* expresses the ultimate in proximity, intimacy, and identity. When Jeremiah speaks of "keepers of my *se-lah* (rib)," he means bosom friends, inseparable companions. Such things are to be taken figuratively, as in Moses 3:22 and Genesis 2:22, when we are told not that the woman was made out of the rib or from the rib, but that she *was* the rib, a powerful metaphor. So likewise "bone of my bone, flesh of my flesh" (Genesis 2:23), "And they shall cleave together as one flesh"—the condition is that of total identity. "Woman, because she was taken out of man" (Moses 3:23) is interesting because the word *woman* is here mysteriously an extension of man, a form peculiar to English; what the element *wo-* or *wif-* means or where it came from remains a mystery according to the *Oxford English Dictionary*. Equally mysterious is the idea of the man and woman as the apple of each other's eye. Philological dictionaries tell us that it is a moot question whether the word *apple* began with the eye or the fruit. The Greek word is *kora* or *korasion,* meaning a little girl or little woman you see in the eye of the beloved; the Latin equivalent is *pupilla,* from *pupa* or *little doll,* from which we get our word *pupil.* What has diverted me to this is the high degree to which this concept is developed in Egypt in the earliest times. The Eye of Re is his daughter, sister, and wife—he sees *himself* when he looks into her eye, and the other way around. It is the image in the eye which is the ideal, the *wdat,* that which is whole and perfect. For "it is not good that man should be alone"; he is incomplete by himself—"the man is not without the *woman* in the Lord."

The perfect and beautiful union of Adam and Eve excited the envy and jealousy of the Evil One, who made it his prime objective to break it up. He began by making both parties self-conscious and uncomfortable. "Ho, ho," said he, "you are naked. You had better run and hide, or at least put something on. How do you think you look to your Father?" They had reason to be ashamed, because their nakedness betrayed their disobedience. They had eaten of the forbidden fruit. But Satan wanted to shock them with his pious show of prudish alarm—he had made them ashamed of being seen together, and that was one wedge driven between them.

His first step (or wedge) had been to get one of them to make an important decision without consulting the other. He approached Adam in the absence of Eve with a proposition to make him wise, and being turned down then sought out the woman to find her alone and thus undermine her resistance more easily. It is important that he was able to find them both alone, a point about which the old Jewish legends have a good deal to say. The tradition is that the two were often apart in the Garden engaged in the separate tasks to which each was best fitted. In other words, being one flesh did not deprive either of them of individuality or separate interests and activities.

After Eve had eaten the fruit and Satan had won his round, the two were now drastically separated, for they were of different natures. But Eve, who in ancient lore is the one who outwits the serpent and trips him up with his own smartness, defeated this trick by a clever argument. First she asked Adam if he intended to keep all of God's commandments. Of course he did! *All* of them? Naturally! And what, pray, was the first and foremost of those commandments? Was it not to multiply and replenish the earth, the universal commandment given to all God's creatures? And how could they keep that commandment if they were separated? It had undeniable priority over the commandment not to eat the fruit. So Adam could only admit that she was right and go along: "I see that it *must* be so," he said, but it was she who made him see it. This is much more than a smart way of winning her point, however. It is the clear declaration that man and woman were put on the earth to stay together and have a family—that is their first obligation and must supersede everything else.

Now a curse was placed on Eve, and it looked as if she would have to pay a high price for taking the initiative in the search for knowledge. To our surprise the *identical* curse was placed on Adam also. For Eve, God "will greatly multiply thy sorrow and thy conception. In sorrow shalt thou bring forth children." The key is the word for sorrow, *tsavadh,* meaning to labor, to toil, to sweat, to do something very hard. To *multiply* does not mean to add or increase but to repeat over and over again; the word in the Septuagint is *plethynomai,* as in the multiplying of words in the repetitious prayers of the ancients. Both the conception and the labor of Eve will be multiple; she will have many children. Then the Lord says to Adam, "In *sorrow* shalt thou eat of it all the days of thy life" (i.e., the bread which his labor must bring forth from the earth). The identical word is used in both cases, the root meaning is to work hard at cutting or digging; both the man and the woman must sorrow and both must labor. (The Septuagint word is *lype,* meaning bodily or mental strain, discomfort, or affliction.) It means not to be sorry, but to have a hard time. If Eve must labor to bring forth, so too must Adam labor (Genesis 3:17; Moses 4:23) to quicken the earth so it shall bring forth. Both of them bring forth life with sweat and tears, and Adam is not the favored party. If his labor is not as severe as hers, it is more protracted. For Eve's life will be spared long after her child-bearing—"nevertheless thy life shall be spared"—while Adam's toil must go on to the end of his days: "In sorrow shalt thou eat of it *all* the days of thy life!" Even retirement is no escape from that sorrow. The thing to notice is that Adam is not let off lightly as a privileged character; he is as bound to Mother Earth as she is to the law of her husband. And why not? If he was willing to follow her, he was also willing to suffer with her, for this affliction was imposed on Adam expressly "because thou hast hearkened unto thy wife and hast partaken of the fruit."

And both their names mean the same thing. For one thing they are both called Adam: "And he called *their* name Adam" (Genesis 3:20; italics added). We are told in the book of Moses that *Adam* means "many," a claim confirmed by recent studies of the Egyptian name of Atum, Tem, Adamu. The same applies to Eve, whose epithet is "the mother of *all* living."

And what a woman! In the Eden story she holds her own as a lone woman in the midst of an all-male cast of no less than seven supermen and angels. Seven males to one lone woman! Interestingly enough, in the lost and fallen world that reverses the celestial order, the ratio is also reversed, when seven women cling to one righteous man. This calls for an explanation: God commanded his creatures to go into the world "two and two," and yet we presently find the ancient patriarchs with huge families and many wives. What had happened? To anticipate our story, it so happened that when the first great apostasy took place in the days of Adam and Eve, the women, being wise after the nature of Mother Eve, were less prone to be taken in by the enticements of the Cainite world. For one thing they couldn't—they were too busy having children to get into all that elaborate nonsensical mischief. Seven women could see the light when only one man could.

The numerical imbalance in the Garden is caused by the presence of all the male heavenly visitors on the scene. Why are all the angels male? Some very early Christian writings suggest an interesting explanation. In the earliest Christian poem, "The Pearl," and in recently discovered Mandaean manuscripts (the Berlin Kephalia), the Christian comes to earth from his heavenly home, leaving his royal parents behind, for a period of testing upon the earth. Then, having overcome the dragon, he returns to the heavenly palace, where he is given a rousing welcome. The first person to greet him on his return is his heavenly mother, who was the last one to embrace him as he left to go down to earth: "The first embrace is that which the Mother of Life gave to the First Man as he separated himself from her in order to come down to earth to his testing." So we have a division of labor. The angels are male because they are missionaries, as the Church on the earth is essentially a missionary organization; the women are engaged in another, but equally important, task: preserving the establishment while the men are away. This relationship is pervasive in the tradition of the race—what the geographer Jean Bruhnes called "the wise force of the earth and the mad force of the sun." It is beautifully expressed in an ode by Sappho:

> The evening brings back all the things that the bright sun of
> morning has scattered
> You bring back the sheep, and the goat and the little boy back to his
> mother.

Odysseus must wander and have his adventures—it is his nature. But life would be nothing to him if he did not know all the time that he had his faithful Penelope waiting for him at home. She is no stick-in-the-mud, however, as things are just as exciting, dangerous, and demanding at home as on the road. (In fact, letters from home to missionary husbands are usually more exciting than their letters from the field.)

So who was the more important? Eve is the first on the scene, not Adam, who woke up only long enough to turn over to fall asleep again; and then when he really woke up he saw the woman standing there, ahead of him, waiting for him. What could he assume but that she had set it all up—she must be the mother of all living! In all that follows she takes the initiative, pursuing the search for ever greater light and knowledge while Adam cautiously holds back. Who was the wiser for that? The first daring step had to be taken, and if in her enthusiasm she let herself be tricked by the persuasive talk of a kindly "brother," it was no fault of hers. Still it was an act of disobedience for which someone had to pay, and she accepted the responsibility. And had she been so foolish? It is she who perceives and points out to Adam that they have done the right thing after all. Sorrow, yes, but she is willing to pass through it for the sake of knowledge—knowledge of good and evil that will provide the test and the victory for working out their salvation as God intends. It is better this way than the old way; *she* is the progressive one. She had not led him astray, for God

47

had specifically commanded her to stick to Adam no matter what: "The woman thou gavest me and commanded that *she* should stay with me: she gave me the fruit, and I did eat." She takes the initiative, and he *hearkens to her*—"because thou hast hearkened to thy wife." She led and he followed. Here Adam comes to her defense as well as his own; if she twisted his arm, she had no choice either; "Don't you see," he says to the Lord, "*you* commanded her to stay with me. What else could she do but take me along with her?"

Next it is the woman who sees through Satan's disguise of clever hypocrisy, identifies him, and exposes him for what he is. She discovers the principle of opposites by which the world is governed and views it with high-spirited optimism: it is not wrong that there is opposition in everything, it is a constructive principle making it possible for people to be intelligently happy. It is better to know the score than not to know it. Finally, it is the "seed of the woman" that repels the serpent and embraces the gospel: she it is who first accepts the gospel of repentance. There is no patriarchy or matriarchy in the Garden; the two supervise each other. Adam is given no arbitrary power; Eve is to heed him only insofar as he obeys their Father—and who decides that? She must keep check on him as much as he does on her. It is, if you will, a system of checks and balances in which each party is as distinct and independent in its sphere as are the departments of government under the Constitution—and just as dependent on each other.

The Dispensation of Adam ended as all great dispensations have ended—in a great apostasy. Adam and Eve brought up their children diligently in the gospel, but the adversary was not idle in his continued attempts to drive wedges between them. He had first to overcome the healthy revulsion, "the enmity," between his followers and "the seed of the woman," and he began with Cain, who went all the way with him "for the sake of getting gain."

> And Adam and Eve blessed the name of God, and they made *all things* known unto their sons and their daughters.
> And Satan came among them, saying: . . . Believe it not. . . . And men began *from that time forth* to be carnal, sensual, and devilish. (Moses 5:12–13; italics added.)

Even in the Garden mankind were subject to temptation; but they were not evil by nature—they had to work at that. All have fallen but how *far* we fall depends on us. From Cain and Lamech through the Watchers and Enoch to the mandatory cleansing of the Flood, the corruption spread and enveloped all the earth. Central to the drama was a never-ending tension and conflict between the matriarchal and patriarchal orders, both of which were perversions. Each has its peculiar brand of corruption.

The *matriarchal* cultures are sedentary (remember that the mother stays home either as Penelope or as the princess confined in the tower), that is, agricultural, chthonian, centering around the Earth Mother. The rites are

48

mostly nocturnal, lunar, voluptuous, and licentious. The classic image is that of the great, rich, corrupt, age-old, and oppressive city Babylon, queen of the world, metropolis, fashion center, the super mall, the scarlet woman, the whore of all the earth, whose merchants and bankers are the oppressors of all people. Though the matriarchy makes for softness and decay, beneath the gentle or beguiling or glittering exterior is the fierce toughness, cunning, and ambition of Miss Piggy.

The *patriarchal* order lends itself to equally impressive abuses. It is nomadic. The hero is the wandering Odysseus or knight errant, the *miles gloriosus,* the pirate, condottiere, the free enterpriser—not the farmer tied to wife and soil, but the hunter and soldier out for adventure, glory, and loot; not the city, but the golden hoard, the *feralis exercitus* that sweeps down upon the soft and sedentary cultures of the coast and the river valley. Its gods are sky gods with the raging sun at their head. Its depravations are not by decay but by fire and sword. As predatory and greedy as the matriarchy, it cumulates its wealth not by unquestioned immemorial custom but by sacred and self-serving laws. The perennial routine calls for the patriarchal tribes of the mountains and the steppes to overrun the wealthy and corrupt cities of the plain only to be absorbed and corrupted by them in turn, so that what we end up with in the long run is the worst of both cultures.

In this great apostasy a new relationship of men and women is the keynote. Lamech got the same degree of Master Mahan as Cain did. These dire operations entail great secrecy, and Lamech's wives "rebelled against him and declared these things abroad and had not compassion. Wherefore Lamech was despised and cast out, and came not among the sons of man lest he should die. *And thus the works of darkness began to prevail among all the sons of men.*" (Moses 5:53–55; italics added). Thus with infallible insight the book of Moses introduces us into the perennial year-drama, which in the past fifty years has become a central theme of comparative world religion and literature. We cannot pursue this fascinating subject here, except to note that from now on the king in his ambition has to cope wih equally ambitious females. Robert Graves takes us through all the primal myths of the Greeks where this deadly rivalry is the name of the game. "In the archaic religious system," he begins (*Greek Mythology,* 1:28), "there were as yet neither gods nor priests, but only a universal goddess and her priestesses, woman being the dominant sex and man her frightened victim." Not a healthy relationship; but matriarchy and patriarchy *must* always be mortal enemies. Why? Because of the last part of the word, the -*archy*. In Bailly's dictionary the first definition given for the word -*arche* is "beginning, specifically the origin of a quarrel or 'a murder' "; the second definition is "command, power, authority," which is what the quarrel is about. —*Archy* means always to be *first* in order, whether in time or eminence; the point is that there can only be *one* first. To be first is Satan's first principle: "Better to reign in Hell, than serve in Heav'n." Whatever the game, the object is to be Number One.

Why do we lay more emphasis on the Patriarchal Order than the matriarchy in our world today? That is unavoidable if we would maintain a balance between the two. For the matriarchal succession enjoys a great natural advantage which, where it prevails, renders the other all but helpless. There is rarely any doubt as to who a baby's mother is; but paternity may always be challenged. In the end the only assurance we have of a true patriarchal succession is the word not of the father but of the mother, as the Egyptians well knew—*Maat* is the official approval of the mother, without which no dynasty could be secure. To assure a true patriarchal succession therefore requires something in the way of checks and controls on the women; a stricter moral code than that required by the matriarchy, which, as we have noted, tends to become lax and promiscuous with the passing of time. With close rules, safeguards, and vigilant surveillance it was only too easy for the patriarchs to become arrogant, dictatorial, self-righteous, and oppressive. The gospel sets absolute limitations beyond which patriarchal authority may not be exercised—the least hint of unkindness acts as a circuit-breaker, "Amen to the priesthood or authority of that man" (D&C 121:37). Without that sacred restraint, patriarchal supremacy has ever tended to become abusive.

A wonderful insight into the archaic order in the bad days after the flood is found in the book of Ether:

> Now Jared became exceedingly sorrowful because of the loss of the kingdom, for he had set his heart upon the kingdom and upon the glory of the world.
>
> Now the daughter of Jared being exceeding expert . . . thought to devise a plan whereby *she* could redeem the kingdom. . . .
>
> Now the daughter of Jared was exceeding fair. And . . . she did talk with her father, and said unto him: Whereby hath my father so much sorrow? Hath he not read the record which our fathers brought across the great deep . . . an account concerning *them of old,* that by their secret plans they did obtain kingdoms and great glory?
>
> And now, therefore, let my father send for Akish . . . and behold, I am fair, and I will dance before him. . . . He will desire me to wife. . . . Then ye shall say: I will give her if ye will bring unto me *the head of my father,* the King. [Here the younger king, at instigation of the princess, a daughter of Jared, seeks the head of the old king, following the ancient practice.]
>
> . . . Akish gathered in unto the house of Jared all his kinsfolk, and said unto them: Will ye swear unto me. . . .
>
> . . . And Akish did administer unto them the oaths which were given *by them of old who also sought power,* which had been handed down even from *Cain.* . . .
>
> And they were kept up by the *power* of the devil . . . to help such as sought *power* to gain *power,* and to murder, and to plunder, and to commit . . . whoredoms. (Ether 8:7-10, 13, 15-16; italics added.)
>
> And . . . *Jared* was anointed king . . . and he gave unto Akish his daughter to wife.
>
> [Akish is now next in line.] And . . . Akish sought the life of

[Jared] . . . and he obtained the head of his father-in-law, as he sat on his throne . . .

And . . . Akish began to be jealous of *his* son [and so starved him to death in prison]. . . .

Now the people of Akish were desirous for *gain,* even as Akish was desirous for *power*; wherefore, the sons of Akish did offer them *money*. . . .

And there began to be a war between the sons of Akish and Akish . . . unto the destruction of nearly all the people of the kingdom. (Ether 9:4–5, 7, 11–12; italics added.)

And it all began with a woman: *Dux femina Facti.*

According to the oldest mythologies, all the troubles of the race are but a perennial feud between the Matriarchy and the Patriarchy; between men and women seeking power and gain at each other's expense.

With infallible instinct Shakespeare takes us into a timeless world of elemental spirits where a fairy king and queen are found shamelessly bickering over a piece of *property*—a little slave. *Proud* Titania and *jealous* Oberon are playing a silly game of one-upmanship—silly, but with appalling results. All nature is blasted and blighted and the only progeny of the squabbling pair is universal sterility; described in harrowing detail by the queen: "And this progeny of evil comes of us, we are its parent and original!" What dismal parenthood! And it all comes of ambition and greed, to which gods and goddesses as well as kings and queens are prone. As a sampling of what goes on and on and on, take the Olympian creation myth. "At the beginning of all things Mother Earth emerged from chaos and bore her son Uranus as she slept"; the two of them united to beget a race of monsters as "earth and sky parted in deadly strife," which, according to Graves, "must refer to the clash between the patriarchal and matriarchal principles." The giant children revolted against their father, Uranus, who threw them into Tartarus; in revenge the mother persuaded their leader, Cronus, to murder his father; upon coming to the throne, Cronus in turn imprisoned his own sons and married his sister Rhea. Jealous of his children, he destroyed them to keep them from deposing him until their mother conspired with her son, Zeus, to dispatch Cronus exactly as he had his father, Uranus. Prometheus became chief advisor to Zeus, the new king, who chained him to a mountain for being "too philanthropic." On the mountain Prometheus had a conversation with the girl Io, who was fleeing for her life: Zeus had brutally attacked her in his lust, and his jealous wife Hera, to avenge herself in him, ordered that Io should be pursued forever by a gadfly. Prometheus prophesied to her, however, that Zeus, the supermacho tyrant, would fall in turn before a hero descended from Io herself. And so it goes, on and on. There must be a better way, and there is.

It was Abraham and Sarah who restored the state of our primal parents—she as well as he, for in the perfect balance they maintained, he is as dependent on her as she on him. With them were restored the covenants and promises of our first parents. The world did everything to force them

51

apart, and if they had thought in terms of power and gain it would certainly have succeeded. What was it that kept them together? The patriarchal narratives bring a new and surprising element into world literature. In the most brutal of worlds they are unique as *romantic* love stories, in which the female lead enjoys a billing equal, if not superior, to that of the male, with her own name, genealogy, royalty, fortune, and as much bargaining power as the man. True, all the marriage brokerage is carried on by families and dynasties, with ambitious parents and arrogant monarchs trying to spoil the love-match, but God approves of the romance, and for once the dire attempts at substituting family and dynastic business-interests for affection are frustrated. From Abraham and Sarah down through Isaac and Jacob and to Joseph and Asenath, that is the plot of the story.

Thus Pharaoh (Nimrod) feared Abraham's power and priesthood (as predicted by his astrologers) and so first attempted to prevent his birth by putting to death all the male infants born in the kingdom and then by imprisoning him as a child and finally by putting him on an altar from which he was delivered by an angel. Finally the proud monarch surrendered and conceded that the God of Abraham had all the power after all.

It was also a pharaoh who sought the hand of Sarah, the true princess, in order to raise up a royal progeny by her. Upon a royal bed identical in form with the altar of Abraham, she too prayed for deliverance and was rescued by an angel while the king was constrained to recognize Sarah's true marriage and heritage, bestowing upon her regal insignia and a royal escort. At God's command, Abraham humbled himself to ask Sarah as a favor to declare herself to be his sister, eligible to marry another and thus save his life. This is only part of the deference that Abraham had to make to his wife, and it left no place for his male pride. Sarah on the other hand, with equal humility, went to Abraham confessing God's hand in her childlessness and actually begging him to have children by another woman. Can one imagine a greater test of her pride? When both sides of the equation are reduced, the remainder on both sides is only a great love.

Again the Apostasy: recently scholars have compared Sarah with Helen of Troy, and the latter can show us as well as anyone how the romantic tradition of the patriarchs went sour. It begins with attempts at seduction—wanton perversion of the forbidden fruit. Queenly Hera offers Paris power and gain to get the golden apple from him while Aphrodite promises him the ultimate—sex and prestige, the world's most beautiful woman for a wife; as for Athena, she is a freak, invented by the patriarchal interests to expedite their takeover of the matriarchal claims: she was not of woman born, but sprang in full masculine armor from the head (not the heart) of the All-Father Zeus—a very masculine damsel, indeed, who always votes with the male contingency; and of course she is ever-virgin and never a mother. Aphrodite got the award—the golden apple, and procured Paris his beautiful wife, who was already married to an obnoxious male chauvinist, who was a king and a serious business rival to her *new* husband (for the Achaeans and Trojans had long waged cold war for the control of the rich grain-trade that passed through the straits from Russia). It was Menelaus's brother Agamemnon, head of the whole vast conglomerate, who led the expedition against Troy. The opening lines of the *Iliad* show this bully-boy insisting that the hero Achilles turn over to him the fair daughter of the priest Chyses, whom Achilles has won in battle. Agamemnon's claim to the girl is very simple: he is the boss, and he wants her. To the girl's father, who comes to ransom her, he bawls out: "No, I am not going to let her go! She's going to get old and gray in my house, far from her home, in the weaving department, and she's going to bed with me whenever I feel like it. Now you get out of here; don't bug me—if you want to leave in one piece!" That is the kind of a great leader Agamemnon is. Note here that Greek women were treated like captives because originally they *were* captives; when the warrior hordes overran the ancient people of the coast, they subjected their matriarchal society to perpetual suppression, though from time to time the smoldering fires broke out fiercely. It is not surprising that Agamemnon, to expedite his journey to Troy, sacrifices his young daughter Iphigenia to Poseidon. But this gave a moral pretext to his wife, Clytemnestra, as ambitious and unscrupulous as he, to connive with her lover in murdering her husband on the day of his return. For which the son, Orestes, murdered *his* mother and the king who ruled by her sufferance. While avenging Furies pursued Orestes, the gods took a vote to decide whether his avenging of his father justified the killing of his mother. Not surprisingly, the vote split on party lines, *every* god voting to acquit the defendant and *every* goddess voting to convict him—another showdown between male and female. The tie was broken by the vote of Athena, invented for the express purpose, it is believed, of tipping the scales for the patriarchy. She also holds the balance between imperious Zeus and relentless Hera in their ceaseless feuding at the expense of poor Odysseus and Penelope. "Zeus and Hera bickered constantly. Vexed by his infidelities, she often humiliated him by her scheming ways. . . . He never fully trusted Hera. . . . She therefore resorted to ruthless intrigue . . ." (1,53)

In Egypt, Israel lived under a matriarchal monarchy from which they were delivered under Moses. His romantic career parallels that of Abraham to a remarkable degree. The tension between matriarchy and patriarchy begins with the Hebrew midwives refusing Pharaoh's command to put to death all the *male* babies, an order which the Egyptians carry out with a will. Moses is rescued by his *mother,* placed in a reed float, rescued and brought up in the rushes of the Delta swamp by two women, a nurse and a princess-mother (exactly like the infant Horus, protected and raised by Isis and Nephthys in the same swamp of Chemmis). Then he marries one of seven water-drawing maidens, who declares her independence and to whose father (not his own father, but his wife's) the hero always defers. He balks at assuming the role of the pharaoh he has overcome in the sea—and indeed it was not he but Miriam who celebrated the victory over the waters and the rival king. When he turns Nile-water into blood (Exodus 5:9), he is performing an age-old rite reserved to the women of Egypt celebrating the founding of the nation by a woman who discovered the land. He leads the people to a place of twelve wells and seventy palms, the symbolic number reminding us that Sarah figures as a palmtree in Abraham's dream in the Genesis Apocrypha, as Nausicaa does in Odysseus' fantasy. When the tables are turned against the Egyptians, it is their *male* first-born who perish—another blow at male succession. Surprisingly, it is not Moses but his wife Zipporah who circumcises their first-born son and proceeds to rebuke her husband with stinging contempt. Plainly the attempt at patriarchal assertion met tough resistance. The people rejected Moses as their leader even after he had saved them (Exodus 16:2; 32:23) and plunged with a will into the licentious matriarchal rites led by the wives and daughters and their sons under their influence (there is no mention of hubands or brothers), who contributed their gold earrings to making the golden calf. That was Ka Mutef, "Bull of His Mother," who represented to the Egyptians the youthful pharaoh's submission to his mother. While they were singing and dancing in the best matriarchal tradition, Moses ordered the death of every *male* participating in the rites; they were to "slay every man his brother" if he caught him at the party. (This third liquidation of males was followed by a solemn rededication to the patriarchal order: "*Consecrate* yourselves ... even every man upon his *son,* and upon his *brother;* that he may bestow upon you a blessing this day" [Exodus 32:29].)

This apostasy had been one of the fastest yet: "They have turned aside *quickly out* of the way which I commanded them," said the Lord to Moses (Exodus 32:8; italics added). And the specific charge is significant: "Oh, this people have sinned a great sin, and have made them gods of *gold*." (Exodus 32:31; italics added) "My people have *sold* themselves for gold and silver." That, along with total depravity, completes the picture and brings the world order back to normal.

After Moses, the romantic David had his women-trouble, as we all know. Like Aaron he danced in the manner of Pharaoh before the altar, and the queen, looking on, "despised him in her heart." What need be said of Solomon and the ladies? That supermacho male chauvinist met his match in the Shulamite woman, who outwitted the all-wise Solomon and thoroughly humiliated him. A whole epic cycle revolves around Solomon's Benedict-and-Beatrice, Petrucchio-and-Catherine game with the Queen of Sheba, who, as Bilqis (the name designates her as a ritual hierodule), matches wits with him for throne and empire, in which he cheats shamelessly but is beaten just the same.

Years ago I collected some hundred versions of the story. Beginning with the account of how Jacob took advantage of the helpless Tamara, who turned his sin against him and came out winner, I was struck to find a whole line of ancient queens doing the same sort of thing—and usually going under the same name. Thus when Cyprus, having conquered all the world but one country, that of the Amazon Massagetae, ignored the wise counsel of his advisor Croesus and invaded that land, its queen Tomyris trapped him at a banquet, where she cut off his head and sloshed it around in a bag of blood. I do not talk about such things for their sensationalism but for their extreme frequency in myth and history—they form a regular pattern, a constant groundwork for history. In the long line of tragicomic *Odi et amo* ("I can't live with you and I can't live without you!") confrontations, man and woman stage an endless tournament of dirty events with survival as the prize. In all of which there is something very wrong, however much we have come to relish it in novels and TV programs. Can this be the purpose of the marvelous providence that brings men and women together? If we must all live together in the eternities, it can never be in such a spirit.

And so we find the celestial order of marriage resorted to again in the Meridian of Time. From the earliest writings, both defending and attacking Christianity, it is clear that the relationship between the sexes was something very special with them. Outsiders were shocked and scandalized, for example, by the promiscuity implied in the Christian practice of calling each other brother and sister. A more-than-ordinary emphasis on family life is apparent in the warnings of First Clement to the leaders of the church that they are neglecting to pay sufficient attention to their own families and the bringing up of their children in the church. The more recent discoveries of early Christian documents allow us insights into the nature of the teaching that incurred the wrathful criticism of an immoral age that did not understand it all. Thus we learn in the Gospel of Philip and the Apocalypse of Adam how Adam and Eve were united in celestial union before the creation of the world but, upon descending to the earth, became separated, with death entering into the scheme. Christ came to earth, says the Gospel of Philip, "for the express purpose of bringing them together in eternal life. Thanks to him those who are united in the Bridal Chamber will never more be separated." The ordinances here are symbolic, but the images are important models to be followed. Let us recall how often the Lord refers to himself as the *Bridegroom*. The symbols we have here are indeed meager compared with the perfect glory. The things we do in symbols merely hint at things as they are, "for there is glory above glory and power upon power.... The Holy of Holies and the Bridal Chamber, these are the ultimate.... Though sin still enslaves us, when the truth is revealed the perfect life will flow for everyone ... that those who were separated may be united and fulfilled.... All who enter the Bridal Chamber may beget in the light—not after the manner of nocturnal mating.... Whoever becomes a Son of the Bridal Chamber will receive the light ... and when he goes out of the world he shall already have received the true instruction through types and images."

That early Christian ideas of marriage were far from the conventional ones is plain enough from the difficult solution to the problem arrived at in the fourth century, when the ceremonies of the church were widely accommodated to those of the world: "Was the church conquering the world," asks the great Catholic historian Duchesne, "or was not the world rather conquering the church?" The solution was to accommodate a difficult concept of marriage with the practices of the world and to accept that ancient and established copout, celibacy. In the Christian literature of the early centuries, when Christianity was splitting up into many sects, each claiming to possess alone the *gnosis,* the secret teaching of the Lord to the apostles after the resurrection, one reads much of the tribulations of Sophia, who is equated with Zoa or Eve. Once long ago, she tried to become perfectly independent and go it alone. She was *Wisdom,* as her name signifies (the Hebrew *Hokhma*), who is almost a person in the scriptures but not quite. If the woman is life she is also *Wisdom.* Well, Sophia thought she, as the mother of all, could not only produce but govern the universe all by herself; the result was a ghastly abortion. Chastened and terrified, she was rescued by Jesus Christ, the Bridegroom, who reached out his hand to her and took her back again, for he needed her too, and only when the two worked together in perfect accord could God's purpose go forward in the universe. Jesus was born when Caesar Augustus was inaugurating the long line of emperors while his wife Livia was initiating the long and fateful line of imperial wives and mistresses. She poisoned right and left to get her son Tiberius on the throne, not because she loved him, but because that was the way of preserving and increasing her own power—and wealth. (Nobody knew better than the Romans that when the treasury was empty the emperor was finished.) Most of the Roman emperors were murdered by their successors, who in turn were murdered by their successors. Rome's one original contribution to letters was a brilliant and perceptive line of satirists telling us all about life in the Roman world: the theme of course was money and sex.

From the confused jumble of traditions and beliefs of late Antiquity (the heritage of very ancient times indeed), there emerged at the beginning of the Middle Ages such mysteries as the Round Table in which we find rejuvenated the romantic ideal of the hero who is never ambitious for himself, and the Lady pure and holy whom he serves. A more dramatic contrast to the reality of the times (as we see in the ten books of Gregory of Tours' *Frankish History*) would be hard to imagine. What put a quietus to the Round Table was partly the stress and tension of perpetual dalliance under the code of chivalry—if Lynette snobbishly humiliated her knight, so Galahad prudishly denied his favors to the ladies—but mostly the failure was brought on by the jealousy and ambition (personified by the sinister Mordred) that poisoned the minds of true lovers.

Shakespeare has given us a classic study in sex and power in *Macbeth.* There is a beautiful relationship between the lord and his lady, until they both start reaching for power. The moral of the play is that the lust for power and gain inevitably destroys the true and proper nature of the sexes. It begins with the archaic matriarchy—dark, chthonian *Hecate,* no less—who sets three women to trap and destroy the hero. But they are unnatural women: "You should be women" says the hero's companion when he sees them. But what can these bearded creatures be? Full of confidence, the hero brushes them aside, and yet he is fascinated by them—"Speak then to

56

me, who neither *beg* nor *fear* your favors or your hate." Proudly independent, he has already taken the bait and is in the trap. Their prophecies get him all excited, and he writes to his wife, who reads his letter and sees right off that in order to promote themselves she and her husband will have to forget all about their natural roles as man and woman:

> Yet do I fear thy nature.
> It is too full the *milk* of human kindness. . . .

For Macbeth was a *kind* man to begin with (the spark of his former self flashes through from time to time during the play), and the lady was known as a sweet and gentle woman. But now she must get down to business:

> Hie thee hither,
> That I may pour my spirits in thine ear,
> And chastise with the valor of *my* tongue.
> All that impedes thee from the golden round.

It is the crown they are after. Why settle for less? In view of such a prospect, all their former values are violently wrenched in a new direction as a messenger comes in and tells the lady that they are about to have a royal guest—the king is already in their power:

> Come you spirits
> That tend on mortal thoughts, *unsex* me here. . . .
> [She must be unsexed to follow her ambition.]
> Come to my woman's breasts
> And take my *milk* for gall, you murdering ministers.

Already milk again: that is the human side of them; both of them share the milk of human kindness—but they must get rid of it to get ahead. Next, flinching from the murder, Macbeth shows his old human self when he is stopped short by the thought of "pity, like a naked newborn babe." But Lady Macbeth pushes him on by telling him to become a *man*. He doesn't like that: a man is one thing, a monster is another: "I dare do all that may become a man. Who dares do *more* is *none*."

You are wrong, she says: I am trying to make a man of you now. That means going all the way:

> When durst do it, then you were a man, And to be more . . . would
> Be so much more the man.

Then she gets back to *milk* again, and says a terrible thing:

> I have given suck, and know
> How tender 'tis to love the babe that milks me.
> I would, while it was smiling in my face,
> Have plucked my nipple from his boneless gums and dashed the
> brains out, had I so sworn as you
> Have done to this.

Unsexed as a woman, unnatural as a mother—if that's what it takes to get what she wants. And what does she want? Power. She wins the argument:

> Bring forth *men*-children only,
> For thy undaunted mettle should compose
> Nothing but *males*.
> [She is too good to be a woman! Women are weak.]

But Lady Macbeth has her moment of weakness: "Had he not resembled My father as he slept, I had done 't." The next words she cries out are, "My husband!" Later she takes him to task: "My hands are of your color, but I shame to wear a heart so white."

Macduff tells Lady Macbeth he cannot tell her what has happened:

> O gentle lady . . .
> The repetition, in a *woman's* ear,
> Would murder as it fell.
> [It should, but she is no longer a woman]

In fact, someone describes the storming night as "unnatural." So the old matriarchs gave Macbeth the crown, but the whole thing is wrong.

> Upon my head they placed a *fruitless* crown
> And put a *barren scepter* in my gripe.

(The words are significant, this sort of success is fruitless and barren.) Macbeth does have a conscience: "Oh, full of scorpions is my mind, dear wife!" He does not want to involve her in any more murders: "Be innocent of the knowledge, *dearest chuck*" (an almost comical betrayal of how he wanted to think of her still). But at the banquet she is at him again: "Are you a man?" "Proper stuff!" "These flaws and starts . . . would well become a *woman's story* at a winter's fire, authorized by her *grandam*. Shame itself". "What, quite *unmanned* in folly? Fie, for shame!"

The ultimate humiliation is now that he should be like a woman—a silly superstitious woman, a feeble, helpless old woman.

To the ghost he says: "What man dare, I dare." [or I would not face you in the flesh] "Protest me the *baby of the girl*." [this is as low as self-concept can get]." Why, so. Being gone, I am a *man again*.

In his rage and frustration he orders the extermination of Macduff's family:

> His wife, his babes, and all unfortunate souls
> That trace him in his line.

"He has no children," is Macduff's reaction when he hears the news. Lady Macduff says when the murderer approaches,

58

I remember now I am in this earthly world, where to do harm is
often laudable, to do good sometime accounted dangerous folly [an
utter perversion of values]. Why, then, alas, do I put up that
womanly defense?

The young and sensitive Malcolm has had more than he can take and
raves:

> Nay, had I power, I should
> Pour the sweet *milk* of concord into Hell,
> Uproar the universal peace, confound
> All *unity* on earth.

At this point Shakespeare introduces an important but often neglected in-
terlude. To check his raving, Macduff replies to Malcolm that his father
and mother were a "most sainted" royal pair.

Malcolm then says: "I am yet unknown to woman, never was forsworn,
scarcely have *coveted* what was my own" (neither sex nor greed had spoiled
him).

The doctor then introduces talk of Edward the Confessor, the reigning
king of England: "At his touch, such *sanctity* hath heaven given his hand,
[those with maladies] presently amend."

Malcolm follows with this observation:

> A most miraculous work in this good king. . . .
> To the succeeding royalty he leaves
> The healing benediction. With this strange virtue
> He hath the heavenly gift of prophecy,
> And sundry blessings hang about his throne
> That speak him *full of grace.*

This scene sets forth the conditions upon which power may be enjoyed
without satanic corruption—only by those who are totally unworldly; for
one in a position of power the only alternative to becoming devilish in
this world is to be *holy.*

In the same scene, when Macduff learns the news, Malcolm says, "Dispute it like a *man.*"

Macduff replies:

> I shall do so,
> But must also *feel it as a man.*

For the Macbeths, on the other hand, to be a man was to have no feelings.
What does the lady care about such things?

> Fie, my lord, fie! A soldier, and afeard? What need we fear who
> knows it, when none can call our power to account?

Get enough power and you can forget about things like feelings and conscience—what can anybody do to you?

As it turns out, Macbeth's undoing is his contempt of women; the witches, "lying like truth," have told him to do whatever he damn pleases "since none *woman* born can harm Macbeth." What's humanity to him? And he keeps harping on that: no mere *woman's* son can get the best of him!

> What's the boy Malcolm?
> Was he not born of *woman?* What's he
> That was not born of *woman?* Such a one
> . . . Am I to fear, or none.
> But swords I smile at, weapons laugh to scorn,
> Brandished by man that's of a *woman* born.

So everything collapses when it is plain that the sisters have played him a rare trick:

> Accursed be the tongue that tells me so,
> For it hath *cowed* my better part of *man!*

In the last scene the new king calls for punishing "the cruel ministers of this dead butcher and his fiendlike Queen." A woman unsexed as she was can no longer be called human.

With the rise of commercialism at the end of the Middle Ages came a feeling of liberation—a romantic release for love, and a free field for acquisition. The relationship of the sexes became both romantic and calculating.

From Shakespeare's and Moliere's comedies down to Agatha Christie, there is nothing wrong with the beloved's expectations of ten thousand a year. Gilbert and Sullivan got away with exposing the deep and pious Victorian situation by making great fun of its absurdity: "I'd laugh my pride to scorn in union holy," says the fair maid, perfectly willing to forget rank and wealth and marry a poor sailor for love alone—on one condition: "Were he more highly born, or I more lowly." For inevitably it was *not* true love that triumphed, as sentimental audiences made themselves think, but the ten thousand a year.

Actually the situation had not changed for thousands of years. The standard plot of modern comedy was that of the New Comedy, which Plautus and Terence got from Menander, where the obstacle to true love is overcome not by sacrifice, but by the manipulation of a clever servant who gulls a rich old man or woman, or, even more delightfully, by the discovery of a token which proves after many years that the poor youth or maiden was nobly born after all and is the heir to a handsome fortune: so now they can get married because they are *both* rich!

And so we come down to the present-day sitcom (where we can laugh freely at everything but the money) and the heavy prime-time show (crime, of course, with single-minded dedication to really *big* money heavily spiced with the super status symbol—plenty of expensive sex).

Here is a little book one of my daughters has. Let me read what is on the cover, and probably inside it: "The College Survival Kit: Fifty-One Proven Strategies for Success in Today's Competitive College World. Survive and succeed—Don't take chances with your college career." Survival, Success, Competitive, career—the dictionary defines *strategy* as "deception practiced on an enemy." The word is well chosen. No deception is too shameful to use against an enemy, and whatever the game, your competitor—even the reluctant customer—*is* the enemy. What a seedbed of mischief this is! The result of this philosophy in terms of human values has recently been the subject of numerous studies. One of the pioneer studies was S. Whyte's *Organization Man,* which told us how the company man would never think of wooing or marrying anyone not approved of by his superiors. So much for true love.

A recent summary of many of these investigations is Michael Maccoby's *The Gamesman.* The section called "The Head and the Heart" is relevant to our discussion: "A corporate president remarked that if he thought of one word to describe his experience with managers over a period of thirty-five years, that word would be *fear."* (There is the cloven hoof again!) "Why are corporate managers fearful?" Mr. Maccoby asks, and he discovers that if the corporate individual could penetrate to the causes of this paralyzing fear and anxiety, he would find *careerism."* (Can we improve on Satan's formula as a definition for that: Careerism is the determination to reign in hell rather than serve in heaven.) "From the moment a person starts treating his life as a career, worry is his constant companion . . . Careerism results not only in constant anxiety, but also in an underdeveloped heart. . . . The careerist constantly betrays himself, since he must ignore idealistic, compassionate, and courageous impulses that might jeopardize his career."

"Perfect love casts out all fear" said the Lord, but who wants that if it jeopardizes one's career? Satan's promise to split Adam and Eve was accomplished when God declared, "My people have sold themselves for gold and silver."

The few scattered case studies introduced here are merely straws—but they show where the fatal wind is ever blowing. Thinking back, what was Satan's express purpose in inaugurating a rule of blood and horror, power and gain on this earth? It was to breach that wall of enmity which protected "the seed of the woman" from his direct attack. Only the covenants of Adam and Abraham and the Church of God can overcome it. Though nothing is to be gained by men and women in fighting for the whip handle, that disgraceful tussle will continue until God cuts it short in righteousness.

So one must choose between Patriarchy and Matriarchy until the Zion of God is truly established upon the earth. It is that old Devil's Dilemma, in which we are asked to take sides with Gog or Magog as his means of decoying us away from our true dedication to that celestial order established in the beginning.

Except You Become
as Little Children

Naomi M. Shumway

Naomi Maxfield Shumway, general president of the Primary organization of The Church of Jesus Christ of Latter-day Saints, was sustained on 5 October 1974 after serving for eleven years on the Primary General Board. Previous to that, she served in teaching and leadership positions in the Primary, the MIA, and the Junior Sunday School.

In keeping with her love of children, Sister Shumway is active in scouting and is currently a member of the National Cub Scout Committee. In addition, she has received the Silver Fawn award.

A mother of three, she is the wife of Roden G. Shumway.

This address was given on 1 February 1980.

Some years ago an article appeared in a monthly educational magazine describing a study on what had happened to a group of children after thirty years. The statistics were informative and interesting, but it is the double-spread picture of the children that has stayed in my mind.

One side of the picture showed the happy, smiling, joyful, confident children. The other side showed them as adults, with anxious, distrustful, unhappy faces.

I wondered, "What is it that causes them to lose the exuberant, smiling expressions of childhood?"

When the prophet Lehi, in the twilight of his life, gave a final blessing to his son Jacob, he declared, "Adam fell that men might be; and men are, that they might have joy" (2 Nephi 2:25). Then Lehi, in a beautiful discourse, explained that this joy, this eternal happiness, could be possible only through the atoning sacrifice of our Savior, Jesus Christ. Lehi said:

> And the Messiah cometh in the fulness of time, that he may redeem
> the children of men from the fall. And because that they are
> redeemed from the fall they have become free forever, knowing good
> from evil; to act for themselves and not to be acted upon. (2 Nephi
> 2:26.)

The very purpose of man's creation is to enable him to gain joy; it is the object and end of existence.

The process of acquiring joy and happiness began in our premortal existence, for it was there that "all the sons of God shouted for joy" (Job 38:7) at the prospect of coming to earth and undergoing its probationary experiences.

Here in mortality we gain joy only by obedience to gospel law. Indeed, the results of obedience are "righteousness, and peace, and joy in the Holy Ghost" (Romans 14:17). The Prophet Joseph Smith said, "Happiness is the object and design of our existence; and will be the end thereof, if we pursue the path that leads to it; and this path is virtue, uprightness, faithfulness, holiness, and keeping all the commandments of God" (Joseph Fielding Smith, comp., *Teachings of the Prophet Joseph Smith* [Salt Lake City: Deseret Book, 1972], pp. 255-56).

During Christ's ministry on earth, he was asked who was the greatest in the kingdom of heaven. He answered in this way:

> And Jesus called a little child unto him, and set him in the midst of them,
>
> And said, Verily I say unto you, Except ye be converted, and become as little children, ye shall not enter into the kingdom of heaven. (Matthew 18:2-3.)

If we are to become as little children in order to inherit the celestial kingdom, what childlike qualities must we hold onto?

Boys and girls sing a song about Jesus in Primary and Sunday School. And most of you sang this song some years ago. Singing it helps children to learn about the qualities that Jesus declares are important for members of his kingdom.

> Jesus once was a little child,
> A little child like me,
> And he was pure and meek and mild,
> As a little child should be.
> He played as little children play,
> The pleasant games of youth;
> But he never got vexed if the game went wrong,
> And he always spoke the truth.
> So, little children,
> Let's you and I
> Try to be like him,
> Try, Try, Try.
> (*Sing with Me* [Salt Lake City: Deseret Book Co., 1969], B-66.)

Stop and think for a moment of the qualities little children have. Decide which qualities you feel are necessary to hold to and to develop as candidates for entrance into the celestial kingdom.

Jesus gave top priority to the quality of humility, for he said: "Whosoever therefore shall humble himself as this little child, the same is greatest

63

in the kingdom of heaven" (Matthew 18:4).

The scriptures clearly point out that all spiritual progress is conditioned upon the attainment of humility. We are commanded to be humble. In 1834, through the Prophet Joseph Smith, the Lord gave this commandment to the Saints gathered at Zion's Camp: "And let all my people who dwell in the regions round about be very faithful, and prayerful, and humble before me" (D&C 105:23).

In 1837, the Lord gave this admonishment to the Prophet Joseph Smith for Thomas Marsh, then the president of the Quorum of the Twelve Apostles: "Be thou humble; and the Lord thy God shall lead thee by the hand and give thee answer to thy prayers" (D&C 112:10).

King Benjamin encouraged his people: "Humble yourselves even in the depths of humility, calling on the name of the Lord daily, and standing steadfastly in the faith" (Mosiah 4:11).

John Ruskin once said:

> I believe that the first test of a truly great man is his humility. Really great men have a curious feeling that the greatness is not in them but through them. And they see something divine in every other man and are endlessly, incredibly merciful. (John Ruskin, *Modern Painters* [New York: Thomas Y. Crowell and Co., 1873], 3:328-9.)

Humility includes obedience, being without guile, and being submissive to the will of our Father in Heaven.

Another high priority for acceptance into the celestial kingdom is the development of faith. Someone has said that there are more examples of and sermons on faithfulness in ancient and Latter-day scriptures than on any other quality.

King Mosiah admonishes us to stand steadfast in faith. James E. Talmage tells us, "Faith is the secret of ambition, the soul of heroism, and the motive power of effort. . . . Faith is a living, inspiring confidence in God, and an acceptance of His will as our law, and His words as our guide in life." (James E. Talmage, *Articles of Faith* [Salt Lake City: The Church of Jesus Christ of Latter-day Saints, 1973], p. 103.)

Children seem to be blessed with implicit faith in our Father in Heaven. And small wonder, for little children are so tender, so recently come from the presence of our Father in Heaven that the spark of divinity is still apparent as we look into their sweet faces.

I am reminded of Stanley, a young father who now has two beautiful daughters. As a child, Stanley had poor health, and many times he was allowed to live only through the goodness of our Heavenly Father. One night, when Stanley was about four years old, he had an asthma attack so severe that each breath was painful and exhausting. In the quiet hours of early morning, his father held him tightly in his arms and rocked him in the big old family rocker, trying to comfort him and ease his breathing. Stanley aroused from a light slumber, looked searchingly into his father's worried face, and said, "Daddy, how do you expect me to get better when you haven't even blessed me?" At that early hour, his father gave Stanley a blessing. Through the faith of a little boy in our Father in Heaven, Stanley has not had an attack of asthma since that time.

I remember one fast Sunday I heard a ten-year-old boy bear his testimony and thank our Heavenly Father for the great blessing he had received through the faith of his friends and family and the power of the priesthood. As he closed his testimony he said, "I pray we all may have faith."

The Savior tells us, "And all things, whatsoever ye shall ask in prayer, believing, ye shall receive" (Matthew 21:22).

President David O. McKay once said:

> I am grateful for the sweet assurance that God is my Father. . . . I would have [you all] have the trust in Him that a little blind girl had in her father. One day she was sitting on his lap in the train and a friend sitting by said, "Let me rest you," . . . [Then] he reached over and took the little child on his lap. The father said to her, "Do you know who is holding you?" "No," she replied, "but you do."
> (Llewellen R. McKay, comp., *True to the Faith* [Salt Lake City: Bookcraft, 1966], p. 80.)

Just so real should be the trust we have in our Father in Heaven.

Children have the great quality of being teachable. They have minds like sponges, absorbing everything they hear, feel, and experience. It isn't difficult for little children to learn that they have a loving Father in Heaven who blesses them with all the beauties of the earth, who wants them to be good and return to him someday. They haven't yet built up the resistant attitude of adults that gets in the way of learning. Little children are constantly learning, and they have an openness, responsiveness, thoughtfulness, and a curiosity that reaches out for truth.

Dr. Burton L. White tells us tht children learn an amazing amount of information the first three short years of their lives:

> After seventeen years of research on how human beings acquire their abilities, I have become convinced that it is to the first three years of life that we should now turn most of our attention. My own studies, as well as the work of many others, have clearly indicated that the experiences of those first years are far more important than we had previously thought. In their simple everyday activities, infants and toddlers form the foundations of *all* later development. (Burton L. White, *The First Three Years of Life,* [Englewood Cliffs, N.J.: Prentice-Hall, 1975], p. xi.)

Dr. Ruth Lundgren, assistant professor of education at the University of Utah and a member of the Primary General Board, reports on research that shows a child has gone 50 percent of the way in the development of thinking patterns by the age of four, and another 20 percent by age eight. To a degree, the way a child learns is already established by the time he begins school.

Our plea should be the same as the plea of children when they sing,

Teach me to walk in the light of his love,
Teach me to pray to my Father above,
Teach me to know of the things that are right,
Teach me, teach me to walk in the light.
(*Sing with Me,* P-45.)

Richard, a young lad of seven, was impressed with his Primary lesson one day and the sincerity with which the teacher gave it. After Primary he asked his mother, "Why don't we have the blessing on our food?" Having no ready answer, she said, "Why don't you ask your father when he comes home from work this evening?" Upon his father's arrival, Richard took him by the hand and earnestly asked, "Dad, why don't we have the blessing on the food at our house?"

His innocent sincerity touched the father's heart, and the father answered, "Son, starting tonight, we will have the blessing on the food. Can you do it for us?"

Delighted with the opportunity to apply what he had been taught, Richard surprised his parents with a short, touching blessing.

During the meal, the conversation centered around Richard's Primary lesson, and he told about his friend's house where they had family prayer.

"Why don't we have family prayer?" he asked. "Our Primary teacher said that we are all children of our Heavenly Father, and we ought to keep in touch with him."

After Richard had gone to bed, the parents began to evaluate their family life.

Next morning before breakfast, the boy's father said, "Richard, Mother and I think you're right. We are children of our Heavenly Father, and we ought to keep in touch with him. Today we will start having family prayer."

Isaiah says, "And a little child shall lead them" (Isaiah 11:6).

We who are older must have the teachable quality of little children as we strive to keep all the commandments and invite the Holy Ghost into our daily lives.

Honesty is another trademark of early childhood. But something seems to happen to the quality of honesty as birthdays pile up. Remember the story we learned in grade school of the Greek patriot, Demosthenes, who traveled the countryside in the daylight with his lantern lighted trying to find one honest man.

Children are often embarrassingly honest. Mark was almost four years old, the youngest in the family and also their delight. The home teachers visiting the family one evening noticed that Mark was not feeling well. He lay on the couch with his head in his mother's lap. Courteously, they said that they wouldn't stay long. The message they brought was enjoyable, but the conversation afterward was a bit lengthy for a little boy who was ill. Completely without guile the little child looked at the home teacher and said softly, "I thought you said you wouldn't stay very long."

Honesty must be high on our list of priorities. Honesty implies freedom from lying, stealing, cheating, and bearing false witness. The Lord categorizes liars with adulterers, whoremongers, and sorcerers. In the Doctrine and Covenants he says: "These are they who suffer the wrath of God on earth" (D&C 76:104).

Stephen L. Richards, who was at one time a member of the First Presidency of the Church, said, "We cannot be Latter-day Saints without being honest; honest with ourselves, honest with our neighbors, honest with our country, honest with God." (Stephen L. Richards, *Where is Wisdom?*, [Salt Lake City: Deseret Book Co., 1955].)

And of course the thirteenth Article of Faith begins: "We believe in being honest, true, chaste, benevolent, virtuous, and in doing good to all men. . . ."

We believe in being honest. We need to practice what we believe.

The Lord gives top priority to the quality of humility, but the great quality of love also has a high priority. What an unforgettable example is given us by children. They love without reservation—open, trusting, with a quick forgiving that is overwhelming.

> Pat and Peggy were glad they were twins so they didn't have to be alone in the new school. They talked often of the fun they had had at school before their Father's work had made it necessary for them to move into a strange big city.
>
> Sadly, they talked to their father about their unfriendly treatment at school. Their wise father listened attentively and then, with a twinkle in his eyes said, "I know what let's do. Let's have a party."
>
> "Who can we invite to a party? We haven't any friends," the twins replied.
>
> Father answered, "Oh, we won't worry about involving friends right now. We'll have an Enemy Party."
>
> Almost everyone who was invited to the party came. When they left they all declared it was the best party they'd ever attended.
>
> Pat and Peggy never did have another Enemy Party. They wouldn't have known anyone to invite because, almost as if by magic, they had only friends in their new school. (A true story retold by Lucille G. Reading, "An Enemy Party," *The Children's Friend*, February 1970, p. 37.)

Over and over our Savior said, "A . . . commandment I give unto you, That ye love one another" (John 13:30). His gospel is a gospel of love. Many attributes and feelings are embraced in gospel love: devotion, adoration, reverence, tenderness, mercy, compassion, grace, service, solicitude, gratitude, kindness. Love's chief manifestation is seen in the grace of God as evidenced in the infinite and eternal atonement.

"For God so loved the world, that he gave his only begotten Son, that whosoever believeth in him should not perish but have everlasting life" (John 3:16; see also D&C 34:3). Infinite and limitless is the love of God, as manifest through the creation and redemption of all things. The Apostle

John aptly crowned his own teachings on love by saying, "God is love" (1 John 4:8). That is, the fulness of perfect love is embodied in him.

For a moment, picture yourselves among the many individuals whom Jesus served—the lame, the deaf, the blind. Such an outpouring of love they felt for the Savior, and he for them. They shed tears of joy as he touched their hearts with his comforting words. He likewise felt of their spirit and was filled with compassion and mercy toward them. As he looked over the multitude, he said,

> Have ye any that are sick among you? Bring them hither. Have ye any that are lame, or blind, or halt, or maimed, or leprous, or that are withered, or that are deaf, or that are afflicted in any manner? Bring them hither and I will heal them . . . for I see that your faith is sufficient that I should heal you. (3 Nephi 17:7–8.)

So they brought their afflicted, their lame, their blind, and their dumb; and he healed them, every one. And all who were there, those who were healed and those who were whole, bowed down in gratitude and praise.

Then Christ called the children around him and commanded the multitude to kneel down upon the ground. He likewise knelt and prayed to the Father. The record reads:

> And no tongue can speak, neither can there be written by any man, neither can the hearts of men conceive so great and marvelous things as we both saw and heard Jesus speak; and no one can conceive of the joy which filled our souls at the time we heard him pray for us unto the Father.
>
> . . . When Jesus had made an end of praying unto the Father, he arose; but so great was the joy of the multitude that they were overcome.
>
> And . . . Jesus . . . bade them arise.
>
> . . . And he said unto them: Blessed are ye because of your faith. And now behold, my joy is full.
>
> And when he had said these words, he wept, . . . and he took their little children, one by one, and blessed them, and prayed unto the Father for them.
>
> And when he had done this he wept again. (3 Nephi 17:17–22.)

Humility, faithfulness, being teachable, being honest, and loving—these are some of the attributes of little children. These are some of the qualities that we, as daughters of God, should have as our priorities, that we must earnestly hold fast to as we grow. For our Savior has told us, "Except ye . . . become as little children, ye shall not enter the kingdom of heaven."

Daughters of God

Elaine A. Cannon

Elaine A. Cannon, wife of D. James Cannon, is the mother of six children and is a nation-ally acclaimed leader, author, and speaker.

She is currently serving as general president of the Young Women's organization of The Church of Jesus Christ of Latter-day Saints. Previous callings have been on the Young Women's General Board, Youth Correlation Committee, LDS Student Association, Church General Activities Committee and Coordinator of the Church's Sesquicentennial Committee.

Sister Cannon has written for the media, both locally and nationally and has authored many books, the most recent of which are: The Summer of My Content, The Mighty Change and Putting Life in Your Story.

As a speaker, Elaine Cannon has been equally successful. She gives continuing education lectures for several universities in Utah and has been presented the Outstanding Teacher of the Year Award for Continuing Education faculty at BYU. Most recently, she was named to the International Platform Association.

This address was given at the Saturday morning devotional service, 2 February 1980.

It has been said that the finest compliment that can be paid to a woman of sense is to address her as such. I do compliment you as women of great sense and sensitivity. It is truly a privilege to cross hearts with you today. It also has been said that "Next to God we are indebted to woman, first for life itself, and then for making it worth living" (*New Dictionary of Thoughts,* [New York: Standard Book Co., 1954], p. 707). I pray that we will all be more excited and more excellent at making life better following this great Women's Conference.

At a world's fair, treasured art was featured in two pavilions sponsored by religious organizations. One exhibit included Michelangelo's haunting *Pieta*—Christ crucified, lying across the lap of grief-stricken Mary.

The Mormon exhibit featured Thorvaldsen's incredibly compelling *Christus*—the risen Lord with his arms outstretched, showing his nail-pierced hands to the multitudes who would come unto him. I learned a powerful lesson about attitude when I overheard a guide explain to a tour group, "This religious group has the dead Christ, and the Mormons have the risen Savior."

One looks at the work of artists through the centuries who have dealt with the nativity—Mary, Joseph, and the baby Jesus. How different they appear when seen through a variety of artist's eyes. The artists deal with the same people and the same tender theme, but their interpretations vary from ornately robed and haloed figures to simply sketched suggestions of the Holy Happening.

We look at ourselves—Mormon women all bound together by church affiliation and similar standards—yet how different we are!

Day by day I deal with these differences in women in the way they see things and what this does to their lives. The weeks are filled now with interviews and moments of counseling, with letters and conversations with women who struggle to work out personal salvation according to their own views of prophets, principles, and problems.

Oh, how we differ. Our roots and the sum of our memories mark us. Sometimes the anguish of the struggle is more painful than pain itself. Sometimes, for a while, confusion rules. Sometimes people are only *convinced* the gospel is true. They are not yet converted.

As I look at you, I see such a cross section. This makes our sociality here interesting as well as challenging. It is recorded in the Doctrine and Covenants, "And that same sociality which exists among us here will exist among us there, only it will be coupled with eternal glory, which glory we do not now enjoy" (D&C 130:2).

Since this is so, should we not now love each other more and not be angry or judgmental over differences? I sense some anger.

The things that matter most must not be sacrificed for those that matter least. It seems to me that it is time, then, for the women of the church to behave with a sense of belonging instead of a sense of separateness.

We are not women of the world, after all. We are sisters. We are daughters of God. We are children of the covenant who are marching to the same drummer though we may be singing a separate song. Matthew Arnold wrote this truth: "Such a price the Gods exact for song: To become what we sing" (Matthew Arnold, *Poems* [London: Macmillan and Co., 1894], p. 34).

As we spend this time together, may we find something that will help us as we sing our songs and live our lives, help us in our similarities as well in our differentness, in our public and private problems, and in our copings and our contributions.

May the spirit of the Lord, whom I love and bear witness of, fill us with love, with joy, and with understanding so that we may feel close to each other and be moved to become more like him.

Sisters, one powerful alikeness we share is the inimitable hope and promise we enjoy through affiliation with this, his church on earth. I am sure you agree. It is like the world's fair, whether we see things as Michelangelo or as Thorvaldsen, we are concerned with Christ. How we look at life will be affected by how we consider Christ.

Being a member of The Church of Jesus Christ of Latter-day Saints took on a new importance to me a few years ago. Before the Washington Temple was closed to the public and dedicated for its sacred service, I wandered through on tour.

The day was gorgeous, colors were rampant in the surrounding woods, and the building was breathtaking with pristine spires rising to the sky. And the spirit there was surging. I was excited and grateful to be there. Everyone else was curious. Washington, D.C., is home for people from all over the world who staff the embassies based there, and hundreds of people with wide-ranging national backgrounds came, some in family groups. There were service people of high rank with their aides dusting the paths ahead and professional people in the arts hiding behind dark glasses. Each looked different, but all reacted similarly. They were thoughtful. They were touched. There were searching questions in discussions with missionaries after. They took every brochure they were offered. They bought copies of the Book of Mormon eagerly. They wanted to buy replicas of what they called the angel "Gabriel." (They hadn't heard of Moroni.) There were none for sale, of course.

One handsome young Scandinavian ski pro with sun-streaked hair and a hand-knit turtleneck sweater stood next to us as we silently toured the last section of the building. The final room housed the white baptismal font resting on twelve oxen. He looked hurriedly about as we went into the room and asked, "Where can I find out more about this church?" Swiftly to his side came several who knew just how to tell him more.

A distinguished-looking gentleman standing by me before the baptismal font said, "I feel I am being guided or swept into something beyond my control—something very deep and wonderful. I've never had a feeling like this. What do I have to do to get in there?" He pointed toward the twelve oxen silently supporting the font.

"Die," I replied.

The Mormons nearby laughed, of course, while I quickly went on to tell him about baptism for the dead and for the living. We talked of repentance and faith, of how Christ died for us and came forth that we might not have to suffer the spiritual death that our serious mistakes—our sins—impose. We talked of not feeling clean enough to meet the Savior if that were suddenly to happen tomorrow. He shook his head sadly.

"I'm not good enough," he said. "If I could just start over. I just don't feel clean enough inside."

I explained the symbolism of the ordinance of baptism—of being buried in the water and coming forth a new being, of being washed clean in the process. Being a man whose business is with people and the symbols used to motivate them, he understood at once and said, "Sprinkling just doesn't do it, does it?"

71

Then we took him to talk with the missionaries.

Sprinkling may not do it, but neither does perfunctory performance or casual acceptance of the vital ordinance of baptism. And so I am going to talk with you about baptism today—about baptism and confirmation and the laying on of hands for the gift of the Holy Ghost and of covenants, commitments, the sacrament, disciplines, freedoms, light, and love. I'm going to talk about taking upon us the name of Jesus Christ and what that means to us as women in The Church of Jesus Christ of Latter-day Saints.

Every woman of whatever age, including the precious little sisters eight and over, should thoroughly understand the sacred act of baptism. Mothers, grandmothers, aunts, babysitters, and special friends of children can teach the blessing of baptism better if they understand it. To our non-member friends we can be eternally helpful if we can properly explain the purpose and symbolism of baptism and testify of him whose name we take upon us when the ordinance is performed.

We talk of these things today because they are the very basis of our lives, the basis of Christ's doctrine for us. In a climate where some barter their Church membership for political expediency or for a moment's pleasure in sin, or who forfeit church-related blessings because they do not fully understand yet, it is well for us to review these things again save we, too, fall. Understanding brings more appropriate behavior. We will be more valiant. We will give more willingly and serve more compassionately and effectively. We will love better.

In the first few chapters of Mosiah, in the Book of Mormon, the powerful sermon of King Benjamin is recorded. Those ancient Americans were deeply moved as they listened to King Benjamin teach of Christ, who was yet to be born. And they cried out in one voice that they wanted to make a covenant with Christ and take upon themselves his name. Then King Benjamin said,

> Ye have spoken the words that I desired; and the covenant which ye have made is a righteous covenant.
>
> And now, because of the covenant which ye have made ye shall be called the children of Christ, his sons, and his daughters. . . .
>
> There is no other name given whereby salvation cometh; therefore, I would that ye should take upon you the name of Christ, all you that have entered into the covenant with God that ye should be obedient unto the end of your lives.
>
> And it shall come to pass that whosoever doeth this shall be found at the right hand of God, for he shall know the name by which he is called; for he shall be called by the name of Christ. (Mosiah 5:6-9.)

When the Savior first came to the Nephite people, he spoke of baptism and its convenant act more than a dozen times in one chapter, as recorded in Third Nephi, chapter 11. He said:

> Whoso believeth in me, and is baptized, the same shall be saved; and they are they who shall inherit the Kingdom of God. . . . This is my

doctrine . . . and unto him will the Father bear record of me, for he will visit him with fire and with the Holy Ghost. (3 Nephi 11:33–35.)

We came to earth trailing clouds of glory. We go, one day, to whatever eternal reward is ours. Our creator has given us the principles and procedures to get through life and to guide us back into his presence. His church is the institution, the framework with which the fulness of his guiding gospel may be found and the necessary ordinances performed with valid authority that binds them in heaven as well as on earth.

His church is named after him–The Church of Jesus Christ of Latter-day Saints. We meet in the name of the Lord. We pray in his name. We covenant in his name. We take his name upon us in sacred ordinances. As sisters, what does this mean to us, specifically? What difference does this make in our lives? How does this set us apart from other women in the world–this taking upon us of the name of Jesus Christ?

Traveling for the Church has given me a perspective that has set me thinking about names. We meet delightful women and girls named Tammie, Maren, Carolyn, Susan, Chieko, Lani, Birgitta, Marja, Cheri, Anja. And we have met a whole new batch of little ones named Camilla–proof that the visits President and Sister Kimball make are remembered with warmth and purpose.

There are many little boys named Spencer these days too, all over the Church.

A time ago, we had a party at our home for a special family occasion. We were honored that President and Sister Kimball came. As I was welcoming them, my sister quickly brought her little son over to meet them. "President Kimball," she said, "this is Mark Spencer Cook."

President Kimball bent his knees so that he could look eye-to-eye with this little boy. Then he took the child's hand firmly in his own and said, "Well, Mark Spencer Cook, do you know what I give to little boys named Spencer?"

"No," came a shy reply.

"I give them a dollar. Camilla, do you have a dollar?"

Obviously Sister Kimball is very important to her husband. When she took upon herself his name, Mrs. Spencer Woolley Kimball, she accepted all the delights as well as the vital duties that a wife is entitled to.

Now, though a little girl be named Camilla and a boy be called Spencer, this does not guarantee she or he will be like them–partner to a prophet or prophet of the Lord. But there is, of course, much that can be said for the power of suggestion. This is true as well for those of us who have formally taken upon us the name of Jesus Christ.

As we take upon us his name, we share in it. In return, he endows us with the gifts of the Holy Ghost–with the power to testify of him to others, power to be effective in our service and callings, power to discern needs of our loved ones, power to discern truth from error. And we receive promptings necessary for making sound value judgments in the many facets of our lives. We need only to listen to the still, small voice and cultivate this spirit within us.

Surely we daughters of our Heavenly Father, whether we are young or old, needful or momentarily fulfilled, can better meet the mighty work of womanhood if we have his spirit with us.

I had a tender experience as a young mother that I think proves this point. I had a new baby brought to me for nursing for the first time since the delivery. As I began the motherly task of feeding the baby, I was prompted by the Spirit that this baby was not mine. I love all babies, but if I have a choice, I'd prefer to care closely for my own.

I checked the identification tag, the wrist bracelet, and the name tape on the baby's back. All indicated I had the right infant, but the Spirit told me otherwise. Subsequent hospital investigation of the baby's footprints confirmed that a mistake had been made. The spirit working through a mother righted a terrible wrong.

Now, if we take upon us the name of Jesus Christ, we take upon us the obligation of being obedient to his will for us, to his timetable for the fulfillment of our dreams, to the way he answers our prayers.

When we covenant with the Lord to take upon us his name, we also take upon us the burden of helping mankind in our special, womanly way. Oh, sisters, can't we do better to bring ourselves together in heart and purpose though our activities may vary somewhat? Can we not go forth from this conference determined to help each other draw closer to Christ, as well as endure the daily grind?

It becomes increasingly clear that the work of women in the plan of life is as critically important as is the administrative and ordinance work of the priesthood. We love, we comfort, we create, we nurture, we teach, we right wrongs, and we provide the atmosphere for heaven on earth. The responsibility of birth falls to us. But the bountiful blessings of being born *again* come only through Melchizedek Priesthood ordinances. What a magnificent method for both women and men.

As we grow in understanding of our relationship with Christ, it makes all the difference in how we feel about ourselves, how we behave, how we assess the antics of the spiritually starved, and how we embrace the principles God has given us to live by. Gradually, as we grow, and through his grace, we become more and more like him.

This is a mighty work. It is His work.

I am not only comforted, but I am excited at what I am seeing among the young women and the older sisters across this world-wide church. Though some are disgruntled, there seems to be a new upsurge of wonderful, committed women. Sisters, the wash *is* being done. The babies *are* being loved and trained. Young women *are* standing firm against peer pressure. People are sensitively spreading the good word. Prayers are being offered more carefully and testimonies more expressed fervently. We have in the Church today women of all ages, like yourselves, who are aware, who care. They understand what it means to take upon them the name of Christ. Their lamps are filled. They are ready. They await the bridegroom.

Meanwhile, they are making the difference in the quality of life of those about them. For example, I met a superb missionary who was older than the other elders. I learned that he had had a very troubled past. When I asked how the change came in him, he replied with tears in his eyes, "My mother prayed me straight. Endlessly, tirelessly, she prayed for me." His record of baptisms adds jewels to his mother's crown.

A family with three teenage children had dropped into inactivity in a Scandinavian stake. The home teachers, the visiting teachers, the priesthood leadership had not been able to reach these people. Then a young woman was called to be a class president. Her attitude was, "If I am called to serve, I will serve with success through the power of God." And she was successful. She reached that family; one of them now serves as branch leader for the young women.

A single woman joined the Church under difficult circumstances some years ago. When I talked with her recently she told me of thirty-one members of her family and of nearly thirty others she had helped into the Church. "I told the Lord if I came into the Church I didn't want to be in alone. I've talked more to him than anyone else in these past years. I tell him if he'll open the doors, I'll walk through and get the people."

As wonderful as these and other women like you are, we can all be even better. We need more women who, having been willing to take upon them the name of Jesus Christ, are then willing to take upon them the work he has designated for the sisters.

We need more women who know Jesus Christ and will teach and testify of him. We need women who are studying of the scriptures, as President Kimball has recently urged, who know the word of God and experiment upon the word; women who will move by knowledge and also by faith, who will "be no more as children, tossed to and fro and carried about with every wind of doctrine ... by the sleight of men and cunning craftiness, whereby they lie in wait to deceive" (Ephesians 4:14).

Dr. Charles D. McIver, in an address to North Carolina College for Women, said, "When you educate a man you educate an individual; when you educate a woman you educate a whole family." Brigham Young admitted that if he had to educate either his sons or his daughters, he would choose his daughters because they would influence generations.

In the process of becoming educated, dear sisters, let us grow spiritually in our knowledge of Christ. This is the all-important knowledge. With this knowledge comes changed.

We need women who are more valiant and who are not ashamed of the gospel of Jesus Christ, who can stand up and be counted, who use the spirit within them to discern. These are the peaceful women. Frustration and depression are not part of their being.

We need women who are willing to make a wholesome difference. Robert Frost's often-quoted poem regarding two roads comes to mind. The one *not* taken made all the difference. And isn't this true with Mormon women and the path we choose to take? Someone once suggested that for evil to flourish it simply requires that good men and women do nothing. For good Mormon women to do nothing—to simply bask in their latter-day blessings—seems to me to be a pitiful breach of promise and purpose.

We need more diligent women to love their husbands into gentility or to just love their husbands and children better. If they haven't either, yet, then we need them to open their hearts and extend the reach of their affection and effectiveness to others.

So whether we are named, Maren, Margit, Susan, Helen, Birgitta, or even Camilla, the Lord needs women who will take upon themselves his ways, his will and his work as well as his name.

If each of us will begin to do this with the power that is in us, we soon will notice a mighty change in our lives. Trials and troubles won't get the better of us. The gates of hell will not prevail against us, and the heaven will shake for our good (See D&C 21:6). Our hearts and our homes will be filled with unspeakable love. Our wards will be stronger, and numbers will swell. Good will be done.

You see, taking upon us the name of Christ and then *living* as if we have, *can* make all the difference.

I know the Lord lives. I am deeply grateful that I have taken upon me his name. It makes all the difference in my life.

I love the Lord; I love and honor and testify of him and of our Heavenly Father. I know that the president of this Church is a prophet of God in the manner of Abraham, Alma, Joseph, Brigham.

Drifting, Dreaming, Directing

Ardeth Greene Kapp

Ardeth Greene Kapp is currently the coordinator for Leadership Training Programs in the Interpersonal Relations and Communications Laboratory at BYU. Formerly a member of the Young Women's General Presidency of The Church of Jesus Christ of Latter-day Saints, she is an accomplished author; her most recent work is Echoes from My Prairie. Sister Kapp also lectures regularly for the Church Educational System.

Her husband, Heber B. Kapp, is president of the Bountiful, Utah, Central stake.

This address, given on 2 February 1980, was the concluding address of the fifth Annual Women's Conference.

As we now approach the closing hour of this fifth annual Women's Conference, surely our vessels must be full to overflowing. To Jill Harris and Kimberly Ford and all of your supporting committees, you are to be commended for this conference. A woman's conference at this time, for which the theme of the addresses have been taken from the words of a living prophet, I believe is of historic significance. As we consider the consequences of the admonition from the Prophet, it is sobering, yet thrilling, to realize the Lord's own words on this matter: "What I the Lord have spoken, I have spoken . . . whether by mine own voice or by the voice of my servants, it is the same" (D&C 1:38). And it is my testimony that we can come to know this for ourselves. We need not wonder.

It is from the words of the prophet that the theme and addresses for this conference have been developed. The expertise and the spiritual insight that have been shared during these few days give me reason to believe that we have been privileged to participate in a planting that will bring forth a full and abundant harvest, not only in the lives of the participants, but also in their homes and communities, and even throughout the world. I am honored to be numbered among you, and I feel at this moment a weighty burden of responsibility.

"What is there yet to be said?" one might rightly ask. The posing of

77

that question brings to mind a little quip which seems to fit this hour. "After all is said and done, there is usually much more said than done." We have a text from our prophet on this matter also. Brief but profound, he simply says, "Do it!"

Being in attendance here at the conference is not the doing part. This conference is intended to help tune the instrument. We must now go home to play the symphony. If the purposes of this conference are to be realized, it will be as we each make choices each day to secure our position and prepare to stand with confidence against the winds that blow, for surely they will.

Of our day, Elder Bruce R. McConkie has said, "Great trials lie ahead. All of the sorrows and perils of the past are but a foretaste of what is yet to be. And we must prepare ourselves temporally and spiritually." (*Ensign,* May 1979, p. 92.) And even with the reality of that kind of a backdrop, President Spencer W. Kimball admonishes us, "Make no small plans, for they hold no magic to stir men's souls" (Regional Representatives Seminar, 1979). It reminds me of Dicken's *A Tale of Two Cities.* The story begins with the contrasts of that day:

> It was the best of times, it was the worst of times; it was the age of wisdom, it was the age of foolishness; it was the epic of belief, it was the epic of incredulity; it was the season of light, it was the season of darkness; it was the spring of hope, it was the winter of despair; we had everything before us, we had nothing before us; we were all going direct to heaven, we were all going direct the other way—in short—the period was so far like the present period, that some of its noisiest authorities insisted on it being received for good or for evil in a superlative degree of comparison only . . . It was the year of our Lord one thousand seven hundred and seventy-five.

And now in the year of our Lord one thousand nine hundred and eighty, the beginning of a new decade, we are living in the times spoken of in the scriptures when peace shall be taken from the earth. Of our time the prophet has said: "To be a righteous woman is a glorious thing in any age. To be a righteous woman during the winding-up scenes on this earth before the Second Coming of our Savior is an especially noble calling. The righteous woman's strength and influence today can be ten-fold what it might be in more tranquil times." (Spencer W. Kimball, *My Beloved Sisters* [Salt Lake City: Deseret Book Co., 1979], p. 17.) Each of us will determine whether this day spoken of as the great and dreadful day will be recorded in our journal of life as a truly great and glorious day in which we are privileged to take part, or if, in fact, it is recorded only as a day of turmoil, conflict, and confusion.

In 1970, President Harold B. Lee was referring to our day, I believe, when he said:

> We have some tight places to go before the Lord is through with this Church and the world in this dispensation, which is the last dispensation which shall usher in the coming of the Lord. The gospel

was restored to prepare a people ready to receive Him. There will be inroads within the Church. There will be, as President Tanner has said, hypocrites—those professing but secretly are full of dead men's bones. We will see those who profess membership, but secretly are plotting and trying to lead people not to follow the leadership that the Lord has set up to preside in this Church.

And knowing the nature of man, the prophet continues, speaking as a seer:

> You may not like what comes from the authority of the Church. It may contradict your political views, it may contradict your social views, it may interfere with some of your social life, but if you listen to these things as if from the mouth of the Lord Himself with patience and faith, the promise is, "the gates of Hell shall not prevail against you; yea, and the Lord God will disperse the powers of darkness from before you, and cause the heavens to shake for your good and his name's glory" (D&C 21:6). ("Uphold the Hands of the President of the Church," *Improvement Era,* December 1970, p. 126.)

It is while one stands undecided, uncommitted, and uncovenanted, with choices waiting to be made, that the vulnerability to every wind that blows becomes life-threatening. Uncertainty, the thief of time and commitment, breeds vacillation and confusion. It is in taking a stand and making a choice to follow our leaders that we become free to move forward. We are then released from the crippling position of doubtful indecision and confusion. We then have access to power and influence, so much so that we can hardly keep pace with our opportunities. It is in or by using our agency and making firm decisions that we turn the key.

Let me share with you a few lines from *The Agony and the Ecstasy* by Irving Stone. On the very brink of creating what for many has become his greatest masterpiece, Michelangelo is faced with a decision that once made must be lived with. He had completed a multitude of drawings suggesting hundreds of ways he might carve the *David.* He had been vacillating, contemplating, considering all the alternatives, the many options, weighing and waiting. Now he must make a choice.

> He burned his earlier drawings, settled down to the simplest beginning, probing within himself. . . . What could he find in David triumphant, he asked himself, worthy of sculpturing. Tradition portrayed him after the fact. Yet David after the battle was certainly an anticlimax, his great moment already gone. Which, then, was the important David? When did David become a giant? After killing Goliath, or at the moment he decided that he must try. David, as he was releasing with brilliant and deadly accuracy the shot from the sling; or David before he entered the battle when he decided that the Israelites must be freed from their vassalage to the Philistines? Was not the decision more important than the act itself, since character was more critical than action? For him, then, it was David's decision that made him a giant, not his killing of Goliath. This was the David he had been seeking, caught at the exultant height of resolution. . . . The man who killed Goliath would be committed all his life to

warfare and its consequence: power. . . . To act was to join. David would not be sure he wanted to join. He had been a man alone. Once he tackled Goliath, there would be no turning back. . . . It was what he sensed that he would do to himself, as well as what the world would do to him, that made him doubtful and averse in changing the pattern of his days. His had been a hard choice indeed. ([New York: Doubleday and Company, 1961], pp. 388, 390–91.)

It was in realizing the importance of David's hard choice and his faith to act that the door was unlocked, allowing Michelangelo to decide about his own mission in marble. Recognizing David as the giant at the moment of his decision allowed Michelangelo to make his decision; and the choice having been made, his tempo changed and with it came strength, power, and hidden energies:

> He soared, he drew with authority and power, he molded in clay . . .
> his fingers unable to keep pace with his thoughts and emotions, and
> with astonishing facility he knew where the David lay. The
> limitations of the block began to appear as assets, forcing his mind
> into a simplicity of design that might never have occurred to him had
> it been whole and perfect. The marble came alive now. (p. 391.)

Each of us must release her own *David* from the imperfect marble that holds it captive, and each of us will greatly hasten that process as we follow the counsel of the prophet. President Kimball has said, "Be wise in the choices that you make. . . . Sharpen the skills you have been given and use the talents with which God has blessed you." (Spencer W. Kimball, "The Role of Righteous Women," *Ensign,* November 1979, p. 103.) As we make right choices we are driven by an exhilaration that causes us to hunger and thirst and feel new energies that lift us, like Michelangelo, toward our goal. "When his right hand tired of driving the hammer, he shifted it to the left, the chisel in his right moving with the same precision and probing sensitivity. He carved at night by candlelight." (p. 394.)

I view this conference as an experience that has brought each of us in closer touch with the marble, though imperfect, with which we must work. As we leave here, it will be in continuing to make right choices, decisions, and commitments that we are released to move forward at a hastened pace and lengthen our stride. If we remain motionless on the brink of indecision we allow our voice, our example, our potential for good to be held imprisoned, as it were, in a slab of marble. Our testimonies, our commitments, and our covenants may lie deep inside, but until we can cut away all the debris that obscures this treasure, it cannot be recognized by others or even trusted by ourselves. On the consequences of a vacillating position, President J. Reuben Clark said: "The spiritual and psychological effect of a weak and vacillating testimony may well be actually harmful instead of helpful" (in Boyd K. Packer, *Teach Ye Diligently,* [Salt Lake City: Deseret Book Co., 1977], p. 315.)

Of this I am sure, and feel impressed to promise: as we each leave this conference and seek divine direction we will find our own block of marble to be more magnificent, with greater potential, than any of us have yet realized. The prophet has called each of us to be "known as women of God," and when the history of this era is reviewed, it might be said of us, as it was of Queen Esther, "And who knoweth whether thou art come to the kingdom for such a time as this" (Esther 4:14).

Even with these truths and inspiring examples before us, I feel concern for some who may leave this conference with a feeling of indigestion—too much, too fast—feeling discouraged and feeling that we get our moralities mixed up with our realities, that the gulf between morality and reality is too big, the stakes too high, the requirements too rigid, and the rewards too uncertain. In response to this earnest concern I have prepared some thoughts that might be considered as we each examine and reexamine our own choices and decisions and opinions in the coming days. In an attempt to give order to these ponderings, I have labeled them, "Drifting, Dreaming, and Directing."

It has been my observation, and it is my confession as a former participant, that many people drift along with the crowd in the Church. Many good people drift to sacrament meeting and Sunday School, even family home evening, and they drift through a casual study of the scriptures. The drifters fall into at least one of two groups: In the first are those who step into the mainstream, getting deeply involved with Church activity and floating with the current, comfortable with a sense of false security that they are in the right place. Others, who form the second group, accepting a few selected principles, resist being part of the flow, the mainstream, and choose to get out into the eddies at the edge, freed from the demands of full participation. It is difficult to decide of these two groups which is better, or worse. Those of us who are, on the basis of activity alone, very much in the Church may not necessarily have the Church very much in us; and if we left, the Church might hardly recognize the difference. Following the practices, doing the right thing but without coming to know, understand, accept, and apply the saving principles and doctrines, we may be compared to one who spends his entire life stringing the instrument—never once hearing the music for which the instrument was created or incapable of recognizing it if he did.

In matters of principle, let us stand as solid as a rock. In matters of practice, may all that we do be based upon these saving principles, and may we understand the intrinsic relationship of principles and practices. It is in making the decision to follow the admonition of the prophet and to become scholars of the scriptures that we gradually learn the doctrine that prepares us to stand on the rock of revelation and to experience less and less the restless sense of drifting, wandering, questioning, and searching.

There are many good people who are very faithful (and may I emphasize *faithful*) in following the traditions and practices. I'm reminded of a song we used to sing in Sunday School:

> Never be late for the Sunday School class, come with your bright

smiling faces.

The chorus ended with:

Try to be there, always be there, promptly at ten in the morning.

Ten in the morning became a practice, a tradition, for a long time. It was not a principle. Yet there were those among the faithful who felt uncomfortable about change, not unlike the feelings expressed by some today as practices and traditions are modified. When changes come, and they always will, for some it may be a test to survive because their foundation is based on practices alone, without an understanding of the eternal, unchanging principles.

Being faithful does not necessarily develop faith. The first principle of the gospel is faith in the Lord, Jesus Christ. To have faith in him is to know him, to know his doctrine, and to know that the course of our life is in harmony with and acceptable to him. It is relatively easy to be faithful, but faith is born out of study, fasting, prayer, meditation, sacrifice, service, and, finally, personal revelation. Glimpses of understanding come line upon line, precept upon precept. Our Father is anxious to feed us just as fast as we can handle it, but we regulate the richness and the volume of our spiritual diet. And we do this by the same method used by the sons of Mosiah:

They had waxed strong in the knowledge of the truth; . . . they had searched the scriptures diligently, that they might know the word of God. But this is not all; they had given themselves to much prayer, and fasting; therefore they had the spirit of prophecy, and the spirit of revelation, and when they taught, they taught with power and authority of God. (Alma 17:2-3.)

Faithfulness without faith, practices without principles, will leave us and our families seriously wanting as we move closer to that time spoken of by Heber C. Kimball when he said, "The time is coming when no man or woman will be able to endure on borrowed light. Each will have to be guided by the light within himself. If ye do not have it, you will not stand." (Quoted by Harold B. Lee, in *Conference Report*, October 1955, p. 56.)

May we find ourselves doing less and less drifting as we make right choices based on personal revelation that give direction to us and our families each day of our life. And with that direction, let us develop "a program for personal improvement . . ." that will cause us to "reach for new levels of achievement," as the prophet has admonished us (See Spencer W. Kimball, *My Bloved Sisters*, p. 20).

He has also promised us that the Lord "will help us from day to day on the allocation of our time and talent. We will move faster if we hurry less. We will make more real progress if we focus on the fundamentals." ("Let Us Move Forward and Upward," *Ensign*, May 1979, p. 83.) Certain principles are essential in our struggle to avoid the wasteful experience of drifting.

Now what of dreamers? Many of us are dreamers at times, wanting in some way to escape ourselves, to be free of our own limitations. I often ponder the words: "With voluntary dreams they cheat their minds." It has been said that if fate would destroy a man, it would first separate his forces and drive him to think one way and act another. It would rob him of the contentment that comes only from unity within. Choices must be decisive so that dreams and actions can be in harmony with each other. When we do something different than we know we should, it is like going into a final examination and putting down the wrong answer, even though we know the right one.

Dreaming, however, can also serve a very positive function when it fits Webster's definition of having "a goal or purpose ardently desired."

In the popular musical *South Pacific,* is the delightful little song that goes, "If you don't have a dream, How ya gonna make a dream come true?" I am concerned for some of our sisters who have a magnificent dream but who will never fully realize its fulfillment because they feel that their righteous husband will take care of it, and they fail to prepare for their part in this eternal partnership.

There are some sisters who ponder the administrative structure of the Church and trouble themselves with what they think they don't have without ever coming to a full understanding of their own special and unique mission and the great blessings reserved specifically for them. We hear it expressed in terms that suggest that because women don't have the priesthood they are shortchanged.

There are still others of our sisters who have the misunderstanding that priesthood is synonymous with men, and so they excuse themselves and have no concern for studying its importance in their own lives. The term *priesthood* is used without qualification, whether it is referring to a bearer of the priesthood, priesthood blessings, or priesthood ordinances. Our hearts should cry out in either case, and we should raise our voices and shout warnings to sisters whose dreams are built on such faulty foundations.

Our greatest dreams will be fulfilled only as we come to understand fully and experience the blessings of the priesthood, the power of the priesthood, and the ordinances of the priesthood in our own lives. If we were to begin with the time a child is given a name and a blessing and then continue on through baptism, confirmation, the sacrament, callings and being set apart, patriarchal blessings, administrations, the endowment, and finally celestial marriage, we would quickly realize that all the saving blessings of the priesthood are for boys and girls, men and women. And while that divine mission of motherhood is paramount, it is not all-inclusive. To help another gain eternal life is a companion privilege. This privilege, indeed this sacred responsibility, this noblest of callings, is denied to no worthy person. To assist in bringing to pass the eternal life of man, and to do it in dignity and honor, is the very pinnacle of my own personal dream. And for us to close our eyes to these eternal truths and not recognize them as priesthood blessings and ordinances is to keep us on the fringe area of the very saving principles—the only principles—that can make our eternal dreams come true.

It is true that as sisters we do not experience a priesthood ordination that carries an administrative function, nor do we have the tremendous, weighty burden of having that sacred responsibility heaped upon us in addition to the mission of creating and nurturing in partnership with God, first in giving birth to the Lord's spirit children and then in raising those children to serve the Lord and keep his commandments.

I have come to know that we can all, both men and women, rejoice in the sacred calling of motherhood. To give birth is but one part of this sacred calling.

After drifting and dreaming, now may we consider the directing of one's life. At my high school graduation, Oscar A. Kirkham stood at the pulpit, looking into the eyes of idealistic, enthusiastic graduates, and in his husky voice he offered this challenge: "Build a seaworthy ship. Be a loyal shipmate, and sail a true course." I don't remember anything else that he said, or what anyone else said, for that matter. But I've pondered that challenge many times over the years. In directing our lives we want to be sure of the true course and its ultimate destination. We cannot risk being caught in the disillusionment of the fellow who was committed to going north and was in fact traveling north—but on an iceberg that was floating south.

"True points," like stars in the heavens to guide us, are readily available for anyone earnestly seeking direction. These true points of doctrine are found in the true Church (See D&C 11:16). Conversion to the truth comes by accepting true doctrine, and the truth of doctrine can be known only by revelation gained as a result of obedience. The Savior taught: "My doctrine is not mine, but his that sent me. If any man will do his will, he shall know of the doctrine, whether it be of God, or whether I speak of myself." (John 7:16-17.)

The skeptic of two thousand years ago might have said, "Look, if I knew for sure that the star (the sign of the Savior's birth) would appear in the heavens tonight, I would be obedient." That's like standing in front of a stove and saying, "Give me some heat, and then I'll put in the wood." We must put in the wood first, and then we feel the warmth and the heat; then we can bear testimony of its reality. In the twelfth chapter of Ether we read: "Dispute not because ye see not, for ye receive no witness until after the trial of your faith" (Ether 12:6). And as our faith is tried and we are found standing firm even in times of storm, we will rejoice with increased confidence as we discover within ourselves the loyal shipmate that we really have as we sail a true course.

Apostles and prophets have been provided in the Church for the purposes of identifying and teaching true doctrine, lest men be "tossed to and fro and carried about with every wind of doctrine" (See Ephesians 4:11-14). Now, we can follow the Brethren blindly, as one of my non-Mormon friends claims that we do—and I might add that it is far safer and better to follow them blindly than not at all—but that could be an abdication of our responsibility to direct our own lives and become spiritually independent. Again, following the practices alone is not enough. We must come to know the reason, indeed the doctrinal bases, for that practice; otherwise, when the practice or tradition is questioned or changed, those who do not understand the principle are prone to waver. They may even abandon or reject the very practice intended as a schoolmaster to carry them to an understanding of a saving and eternal principle.

There were those in King Benjamin's time who were caught up in exacting the law of Moses. With blinders they followed the practices—an eye for an eye and a tooth for a tooth—until King Benjamin taught them that their practices availed them nothing unless they accepted the mission of the Savior and his atonement. Without that commitment their practices were for naught.

While Adam was offering the firstlings of the flock, an angel appeared and asked him why he was doing it, why this practice. You will remember Adam's response. He said, "I know not, save the Lord commanded me" (Moses 5:6). The practice was offering sacrifice, but the principle, in this instance, was obedience. And then Adam received a witness, after the trial of his faith. The angel explained: "This thing is a similitude of the sacrifice of the Only Begotten of the Father" (Moses 5:7).

As we direct our lives, it is important to understand practices and principles, their relationship as well as the differences between them. In my mind's eye, I visualize the practices as a horizontal line, a foundation, a schooling, a testing, a preparation; and the saving and exalting eternal principles or doctrine as a vertical line that links our souls to heaven and builds the relationship with God and faith in the Lord, Jesus Christ, and his mission.

There will continue to be much opposition to true doctrine; but by and by the storm subsides, the clouds disperse, the sun breaks forth, and the rock of truth is seen again, firm and lasting. There never was a true principle that was not met by storm after storm of opposition and abuse, until that principle had obtained such influence that it no longer paid to oppose it. But until that time, the opposition and the abuse have ebbed and flowed like the tide. It was a strong doctrine that rid Jesus of his weak disciples, and the same testing process continues today in determining those worthy of his kingdom. The Prophet Joseph Smith stated:

> God has in reserve a time . . . when he will bring all his subjects, who
> have obeyed his voice and kept his commandments, into his celestial
> rest. This rest is of such perfection and glory, that man has need of a
> preparation before he can, according to the laws of that kingdom,
> enter it and enjoy its blessings. This being the fact, God has given
> certain laws to the human family, which, if observed are sufficient to
> prepare them to inherit this rest. This, then, we conclude was the
> purpose of God in giving his laws to us. (Joseph Fielding Smith,
> comp., *Teachings of the Prophet Joseph Smith* [Salt Lake City, Utah:
> Deseret Book Co., 1969], p. 54.)

In our goal to apply principles and proceed with direction, it isn't intended that we arrive before we experience that witness of the spirit. The witness sustains us in our journey. In a few lines of prose, given so eloquently, President Kimball tells how the gospel came into the life of an unlearned, Bolivian woman. In hearing of the mission of the Savior and the doctrine of the Atonement, the Spirit bore witness to her soul. With her golden-brown face turned upward, her dark eyes wide and trusting, with tears rising to overflowing, she whispered her emotions, "You mean, He did that for me?" With the confirmation of her question received, she again whispered, this time not in question but in reverent awe, "You mean, he did that for me!"

And to this eternal and saving principle, I bear my fervent testimony that he did that for you and for me. With that conviction, I think with soberness of the penetrating observation by Truman Madsen, "The greatest tragedy of our life is that our Savior paid the awful price of suffering so that He could help us, but is forbidden to because we won't let Him. We look down instead of up." ("Prayer and the Prophet Joseph," *Ensign,* January 1976, p. 23.) We choose to remain enclosed in marble. But if we would free ourselves and come to know this truth through personal revelation, the time might come when even our routine practices could become life-giving and done in the Lord's name with his spirit so that the whole of our lives becomes a sacred experience as we labor for him continuously.

It was not long ago that I witnessed what until then had been something of a routine for me, the blessing on the food. Picture with me, my aged father, his body deteriorated by the devastation of stomach cancer, while his spirit was magnified and refined through suffering. He sat at the kitchen table; he then weighed less than a hundred pounds. Bowing his head, resting it in his frail, trembling hands over a spoonful of baby food—all that he could eat—he pronounced a blessing on the food—as though it were a sacred sacrament—and gave thanks with acceptance and submission, with truth and faith, because he knew to whom he was speaking.

It is in coming to know our Savior and the saving principles that he taught through the gospel of Jesus Christ that we become different. And we need to be recognized as being different. The majority of the world doesn't see the options. It is our responsibility to be obviously good and obviously right—and able to articulate our values and be an advocate for truth. We may have a temple recommend and attend our meetings and practice the principles, but how we look and act, what we say and do, may be the only message some people will receive. Our acts should show that there is a power and an influence with us that the inhabitants of the world do not understand. What is it that distinguishes us from others? The distinction is that we profess to be guided by revelation. And it is because of this principle that we are peculiar since all of our actions can be under divine guidance. Having made the choice, we must stand and be visibly different. Until we make that choice, we remain anonymous, subject to the current of the meandering multitudes.

President Kimball has said:

> Much of the major growth that is coming to the Church in the last days will come because many of the good women of the world (in whom there is often such an inner sense of spirituality) will be drawn to the Church in large numbers. This will happen to the degree that the women of the Church reflect righteousness and articulateness in their lives and to the degree that they are seen as distinct and different—in happy ways—from the women of the world. (*My Beloved Sisters,* p. 44.)

That is our direction. That is our challenge.

All individuals are what they are and where they are by a composite of choices that direct their life each day. The responsibility of directing is not only for our own lives, but also for others who may be looking for the light. As we build a seaworthy ship and then sail a true course, many sails will navigate safely through troubled waters into the peaceful harbor because of the unflickering light radiating from the bow of our craft. As I consider our responsibility to others I am inspired by the words of the song:

> Brightly beams our Father's mercy from his lighthouse evermore,
> But to us he gives the keeping of the lights along the shore.
> *Chorus.* Let the lower lights be burning; send a gleam across the wave;
> Some poor fainting, struggling seaman you may rescue; you may save.
>
> Dark the night of sin has settled; loud the angry billows roar.
> Eager eyes are watching, longing, for the lights along the shore.
> *Chorus*
> Trim your feeble lamp, my brother; some poor sailor, tempest tost,
> Trying now to make the harbor, in the darkness may be lost.
> *Chorus*
> (*Hymns: The Church of Jesus Christ of Latter-day Saints* [Salt Lake City: Deseret Book Co., 1976], no. 301.)

Elder Neal A. Maxwell recently wrote, "As other lights flicker and fade, the light of the gospel will burn ever more brightly in a darkening world, guiding the humble but irritating the guilty and those who prefer the dusk of decadence" (*Church News,* 5 January 1970, p. 28).

Now my dear sisters, may our lights be bright without a flicker, as we tend the lights along the shore. Let us each one reach out and touch another. Let us help carry one another's burdens. In cooperation we can overcome great odds. Let us rejoice with one another. It may be just a smile, a note, a call, an encouraging word that says, "I care; I understand; I will stand by you and help you." These are life-saving measures in times of storm.

Recently I was privileged to read part of a blessing received by one of our sisters that stated that her life would continue over a period when she would see great devastation and that she would be called to go into homes of the sorrowing, the suffering, the sick and afflicted, to minister unto them, to bind up their wounds, and to cheer them.

I believe that we have all been called to minister unto those in need, to bind up not just their physical wounds but also their spiritual wounds, social wounds, and wounds that are kept hidden, sometimes festering until someone cares enough to tend the lights along the shore.

These are matters of eternal consequence, and we can, if we desire, reach far enough to experience an awakening of things we have known before. Remember, President Kimball said:

> In the world before we came here, faithful women were given certain assignments while faithful men were foreordained to certain priesthood tasks. While we do not remember the particulars, this does not alter the glorious reality of what we once agreed to. We are accountable for those things which long ago were expected of us just as are those whom we sustain as prophets and apostles. (*My Beloved Sisters,* p. 37.)

It is my fervent and humble testimony that the heavens are very much open to women today. They are not closed unless we, ourselves, by our choices, close them. And this reality can be just as evident as in any time past. As I read of the great spirituality of women of the past and realize how the Lord communicated with them, I thrill with the spiritual manifestations that have accompanied their missions in life, literally a power evidencing the will of God made known through their instrumentality. I think of Eliza R. Snow, of whom Joseph F. Smith said, "She walked not in the borrowed light of others, but faced the morning unafraid and invincible."

The spirit whispers to me that there are Eliza R. Snows among us even today, and there can be many, many more. We can pull down the blessings of heaven through obedience to law. These divine and sacred blessings are not reserved for others alone. Visions and revelations come by the power of the Holy Ghost, and the Lord has said, "And on my servants and on my handmaidens I will pour out in those days of my Spirit; and they shall prophesy" (Acts 2:18).

Now let us go forth with the faith, the vision, the direction, and the decision to abide the laws that ensure these blessings not only for ourselves and our families but for all of God's children everywhere.

As we leave this conference, let us each feel deeply the power and strength and influence for good of our collective and united resolves. With renewed determination and confidence and commitment to the covenants we have made, let us become truly and in every way "Women of God." Let us go forth in faith and confidence and prepare for the noble calling spoken of by the Prophet—to be a righteous woman during the winding-up scenes on this earth before the second coming of our Savior.

Part Three

Mormon Women: A Response to the World

Welcome

Dr. Jae R. Ballif

Dear friends, in behalf of President Oaks, who is in the East, we welcome you this morning to the University, to the Women's Conference, and to this panel discussion. We are very pleased that the participants in this panel are dealing with important questions. They have avoided the temptation to discuss the more foolish and unlearned questions which, as Paul taught, "only gender strife." They will explore, instead, the more profound questions, wise and learned questions, that will lead to understanding and peace. That is the fundamental purpose of the University. It is not enough to be understood, though it is comforting. We must all understand what is true and what that truth compels us to do.

In the last issue of the *Chronicle of Higher Education,* I read with alarm a report stating that in the past ten years there has been a dramatic change in the career goals of freshman women. In just ten years, investigator have found that:

1. Being very well-off financially was cited by 28 percent more men, but by 77 percent more women.
2. Recognition among peers was cited by 21 percent more men, but by 41 percent more women.
3. Developing a philosophy of life was cited as a very important or essential goal by 36 percent fewer women and 35 percent fewer men.
4. Raising a family was cited by 17 percent fewer women and 2 percent fewer men.

I believe this evidence to be just one indicator of eroding values among the women of the world who have in the past compensated for so many of the worldly values of many men. In our response to apparent trends, we are sometimes unwittingly or naively drawn into discussion of unlearned questions that do gender strife.

Today, these noble Mormon women respond to the world by considering the more significant issues. Though there is great diversity in circumstance, talent, and opportunity of these and other Mormon women, we see that there is and must be a convergence on those central issues that lead all who aspire to eternal life to that required oneness with the Savior.

My mother once wrote the following verse:

One day in the morning, when mist lay everywhere, I looked up into the sky and said, "Heavenly Father, Hi."

He heard me through the cloud and answered, "How do you do?" And, "Who are you?"

I was about to tell him my name when he said, "I mean, how do you know that you are you?"

"That's a funny question," I replied, "Because—well, I just know that I am."

He smiled and said to me, "I see."

And in a minute more he said, "Do you want to know who I am?" "I am the Great I Am."

"Oh," I said, "Oh."

That's all we said to each other that day in the morning, but I knew that he was there when mist lay everywhere.

When we finally understand, as women and men, who we really are, what we can become, and the process that begins with faith and ends with change or repentance, all else pales in importance.

Introduction

Maren M. Mouritsen

Unity and diversity—two concepts that on the surface seem, if not contradictory, at least somewhat conflicting. *Unity* implies a oneness, a coming together, a sameness. *Diversity* conjures up notions of options, of differences, of a smorgasbord of alternatives and possibilities.

And yet the participants on this panel, "Mormon Women: A Response to the World," embody qualities of both unity and diversity. Unity, as a group of Mormon women join together to enunciate principles and bases held in common. Diversity, as each reflects both a set of circumstances and individual and, yes, diverse ways of meeting those circumstances.

Panel members were selected both for their commitment to the gospel and for their unique ways, some chosen and others imposed, of fulfilling that commitment in a fairly broad range of life-styles. While the participants' situations vary widely and attempts were made to represent some of those life-styles that Mormon women commonly confront today, no such group could ever be fully representative of all individuals, opinions, or approaches. Our attempt will be to say, both by our verbal statements and by our life experiences themselves, something about our own struggles to balance our commitment and conformity with our independence and uniqueness. This need to balance, this forging of a dynamic tension between our unity and our diversity will form the basis for our discussion here today and for future dialogue.

President Dallin H. Oaks, in a 1975 address, made this significant comment about the struggle for balance:

> My studies and reflections have identified three general positions of
> the roles of men and women. The two extremes, easily defined and
> comfortingly doctrinaire, are both unacceptable in my view. One
> assigns women a different and inferior role in all of life's activities.
> The other extreme, at least partly a response to the historic excesses
> of the first, is the position of the extreme liberationists that any
> differences between the roles of men and women must be eradicated.

The third position rejects both extremes and seeks to find some reasonable middle ground, preserving and honoring God-given differences in the strengths, functions, and responsibilities of men and women, but seeking to eliminate needless current differences or discriminations that are rooted in custom or social mores rather than reason or revelation. Unlike the mindless extremes, this middle ground is difficult to locate and defend, but the improvement is well worth the effort. (Oaks, Dallin H., "Statement On Concerns of Women," *Annual University Conference* [Provo: Brigham Young University, 1975], pp. 29–30.)

One final word: the panel is entitled "Mormon Women: A Response to the World." The title was not capriciously chosen. We acknowledge our position, status, role, or whatever else it might be deemed, as "Mormon Women." We accept and affirm our commitment to the gospel of Jesus Christ. And our response, while as diverse and unique as each of us is, is only one of many responses. There are, no doubt, others that will emerge. It is appropriate and desirable that we each realize both our context and our unique process of living within it.

We submit the comments of this panel as a beginning for opening the dialogue to the wide range of possibilities available to all of us as "Women of God," struggling to balance all that we are with all that we may become.

Happily Ever After ...

Jean Taylor

Jean Taylor, wife of the late S. S. Taylor, Jr., earned a master's degree from California State University at Northridge, where she also taught freshman English. For the past five years she has been teaching English at American Fork High School. Sister Taylor has served as the Chairman of the Secondary Curriculum Conference for the Alpine School District. She has been a Primary president as well as a teacher in almost every auxiliary of the Church. She is the mother of four sons and an avid gardener; in fact, she is reputed to have the most meticulously groomed yard in her neighborhood.

Happily ever after. Yes, that was how I had planned my life—to live happily ever after being a supportive wife and a loving mother. And at age 31, happily ever after seemed to me a reality. Just seven months earlier, I had given birth to our fourth son. My husband, at age 33, after serving as the elders quorum president, as the second counselor in the bishopric, and as a member of the high council, had just been sustained as the bishop of our ward. And now we were on our way to Salt Lake to attend April conference, with happily ever after in our grasp. But then that car came straight at us. The next thing I knew our car had flipped over, the children and I were sprawled over the highway, and my husband—he was dead. My happily-ever-after world was shattered.

Certainly the outpouring of love from family and friends helped put the pieces back together. So many people were willing to give of themselves. There were those who came and finished painting the outside of the house, a job my husband had started just before our accident; those two young men who installed a burglar alarm so we would feel more secure; those loving sisters who brought in hot, delicious meals day after day; those who always had a kind word; those who offered so many prayers in our behalf. All the caring, all the loving *did* help me get through each day. But that was all life was for many months—just getting through each day.

Finding myself in the role of a single parent somehow seemed to destroy all my self-confidence. I had always prided myself in my ability to tackle any job that needed to be done. Hadn't I been the one to handle the finances in our home, to pay all the bills, to figure out the income tax forms; hadn't I done much of the yard work; hadn't I helped with the painting and fix-up projects; hadn't I taken care of the children by myself for many weeks when my husband was out of town on business? Yes, I was independent. Or so I thought. But I hadn't realized how much I, in reality, had leaned on my husband for so many things: for a feeling of security, for a feeling of belonging, and, most importantly, for a feeling of self-confidence. Now I was besieged with doubts about myself. How could I possibly successfully raise our four sons alone? How could I financially provide for missions and college alone? I even worried about the last days and getting us through that ordeal alone. It wasn't long until I was convinced that Heavenly Father had made a terrible mistake. He should have taken me and left my husband, for he would have been successful alone.

Because of these feelings of self-doubt, I found myself more and more on my knees, pleading for help from my Heavenly Father. Miraculously, the answer came, and peace filled my soul. I was important; I was capable; I could succeed. Why? Because I suddenly realized the strength inherent in being the literal offspring of God. I realized that my Heavenly Father truly loved me, that he was on my side—these truths burned within me. I wasn't alone. It was all so simple. My Heavenly Father had confidence in me. He knew I could succeed, for I was a daughter of God.

With the strength of this miracle, I was able to reach out and not just get through each day—I was again able to use each day's opportunities for growth and development. I could once again live more than one day at a time; I could confidently make plans for next week, for next month, and even for next year.

Of course, my most pressing plans concerned financial security. I had graduated from college the year I was married and had qualified for a secondary teaching credential. But I had chosen motherhood as my career and had never taught school; consequently, my teaching credential had expired. Therefore, I decided to return to college and had as my goal earning a masters degree and at the same time renewing my teaching credential. This goal became a reality in 1976, just seven years after our accident. Since my student teaching experience had been sixteen years earlier, I decided that I should repeat that experience to bring me more up-to-date. Dutifully I reported to my assignment, which was at a minority high school in the Los Angeles area and involved teaching one sophomore and one senior English class for one semester. After several days of teaching, my cooperating teacher, with a puzzled look on her face, questioned me about the personal history I had written for her. "There must be some mistake. It says here you have never taught in the public schools." I assured her that was correct. "Then," she asked, "how can you be so at home in the classroom? How can you so successfully reach and teach these kids?"

I thought for a moment and then replied, "Well, I have had many experiences teaching in my church."

It was then I realized the second miracle in my life, a miracle that had been taking place for twenty-five years without my fully realizing it. This miracle was the tremendous personal growth that was mine through activity in The Church of Jesus Christ of Latter-day Saints. Because of my membership; because of my activity; because of teaching those Primary lessons, those cub scout lessons, those Relief Society lessons, those teacher-training lessons, I had unknowingly prepared myself for a challenge in my life that I had no idea I would ever face. Activity in the Church had actually prepared me more fully than had my academic activities to step successfully out of the home and into a career when that step became a necessity.

I thought then of so many other opportunities and blessings church activity had afforded me, opportunities that I would never have had in the world, opportunities for tremendous growth and self-fulfillment. I had been in MIA plays and roadshows; I had even directed a play. I had participated in many sports activities, I had written Relief Society skits, and I had organized ward dinners. But perhaps most important, through church activity I had learned to accept others, I had learned to identify and interact with others, and I had thus learned to reach out and touch lives.

After several weeks of teaching, my cooperating teacher again stopped me with a question. "Jean, what are you going to do with the Mexican kid in the front row?" I looked puzzled; I didn't know who she meant. "Joey," she said.

"Oh, is Joey a Mexican?" I replied.

She laughed. "How is it that you don't see these students as Mexicans, Blacks, or Orientals?

I had never thought about it. "I guess," I replied, "because I see them all as God's children." Because of this feeling, there were no barriers; I was able to reach all the students, regardless of race. And even better, they all reached me; they all touched me. And I was fulfilled. That terrible emptiness left by my husband's death was gradually being alleviated.

Now I am in my fifth year of teaching English at American Fork High School. I detest having to have a job, for I am not the career-woman type. But I dearly love my job. The satisfaction I gain is immeasurable. Being able to help even one student learn one of life's valuable truths through reading a fine piece of literature; being able to help even one student gain power through more effective and more creative use of his language; and, most important, being able to help even one student gain some confidence in himself and his abilities—for I know the value of self-confidence—this is exciting, this is rewarding, this is fulfilling.

My oldest son is now a freshman at BYU in the Honors Program, planning for his mission in May. My second son is a junior at American Fork High School, an *A* student enjoying success not only in the classroom but also on the basketball court and the soccer field. My third son is an *A* student in the ninth grade, keeping busy playing the clarinet and the saxophone, and building and flying radio-control airplanes. My fourth son is in the sixth grade, a fine, exciting student, very gregarious and exuberant, making friends wherever he goes.

Is it possible that because of the miracles of the gospel and membership in The Church of Jesus Christ of Latter-day Saints, my story is, after all, a happily-ever-after story?

A Woman's
Role and Destiny

Ida Smith

Ida Smith is currently the Director of the Women's Research Institute at Brigham Young University. Among the various committees she serves on are the Women's Concerns Committee and the Women's History Archives Committee. Sister Smith has held many Church positions including that of being a cochairperson of multiregional conferences for Special Interests throughout Utah and California. She is a regular writer for Outreach, *a Church publication in the San Francisco Bay area.*

One hundred and fifty years ago the Lord restored the gospel of Jesus Christ to the earth through the boy prophet, Joseph Smith. Through this young man, knowledge and information that had been lost, forgotten, changed, and, in some cases, denied, for nineteen centuries was once again made available to the children of God.

In most cases the inhabitants of the earth were no more ready to receive the gospel in 1830 than they had been to receive it from the Savior himself nineteen hundred years before. As the prophet described it, the vision and understanding of the people suffered because of the "traditions of their fathers" and—I would add—because of their mothers, as well.

The people cried blasphemy when the prophet declared that not only could God still talk to man (revelation had not ceased), but that he *had* talked to him. He was denounced when he claimed that God and Christ had corporeal bodies—separate, distinct, and tangible.

But this was only the beginning of new, revealed truths to come to the world through this young prophet chosen to usher in the last dispensation. And history shows that the world at large was still not ready, able, or willing to receive most of what he taught.

From a tiny core of devoted converts, the Lord sent out missionaries to preach the restored gospel, and as the little band of "Mormons" grew, the Prophet Joseph endeavored to teach and prepare a Zion people that could, one day, teach and bless the Lord's children all over the world.

Many of the revealed truths found unpalatable then still stick in some throats today; but one area of knowledge—hard, if not impossible, to swallow then—is finally, in our day, coming into its own. That area: Women.

The Prophet Joseph Smith did more than just preach that men and women were of equal value and importance in the sight of God. He preached that in order for a man to achieve his highest potential (the Celestial Kingdom and godhood) he must have a woman—equally exalted—by his side and sealed to him forever (See D&C 131:1-2 and D&C 132:4). A just God would not require the yoking of two unequal beings for eternity. Joseph also learned that our Father in Heaven is not single, that we have a mother in heaven as well, that together they reign, and that we are made in their image—male and female (See Parley P. Pratt, *Autobiography of Parley P. Pratt* [Salt Lake City: Deseret Book Co., 1970], pp. 297-98 and Parley P. Pratt, *Key to the Science of Theology* [Salt Lake City: Deseret Book Co., 1978], p. 102).

As temples were built and temple ordinances restored, our knowledge of the eternal values of the male-female relationship has increased. We now know that both men and women share in *all* the blessings of the priesthood and that both share in all the gifts of the spirit (i.e., to heal, to be healed, to speak in tongues, to prophesy, etc.) (See Bruce R. McConkie, "Our Sisters from the Beginning," *Ensign,* January 1979, p. 61). We now know that the man's function in the priesthood is to administer, that the woman's function is creative, and that together they have a perfect balance. As Paul stated, "Nevertheless neither is the man without the woman, neither the woman without the man, in the Lord" (1 Corinthians 11:11).

Marriage may or may not happen during our stay in the second estate. President Kimball said in his talk to women in September of 1979:

> Sometimes to be tested and proved requires that we be temporarily deprived—but righteous women and men will one day receive *all*—think of it, sisters—*all* that our Father has! It is not only worth waiting for; it is worth living for!
>
> Meanwhile, one does not need to be married or a mother in order to keep the first and second great commandments—those of loving God and our fellowmen—on which Jesus said hang all the law and all the prophets. ("The Role of Righteous Women," *Ensign* November 1979, p. 103.)

The important thing for a woman to learn in this life is her eternal role so that when she is sealed she will be prepared and ready—with all her heart—to function in and glorify that role. That means being ready and prepared to function as a full partner in a celestial team—without having to look *up* for help and direction or look *down* because of any feeling of superiority, but being able to look *across* into the eyes of an equally prepared, equally magnificent eternal mate.

Such an exalted role for women was mind-boggling for nineteenth-century America. Here, as elsewhere, not only were most societies male dominated, but men were generally regarded as superior beings. Men were not only to be protectors of women, but they were responsible for the salvation of women as well.

When the Prophet Joseph organized the women after the pattern of the priesthood in 1842, he charged them that from that time forth, they were responsible for their own sins ("Minutes of the Nauvoo Relief Society, 17 March 1842 to 18 March 1844," 28 April 1842, p. 39, Church Historical Department, The Church of Jesus Christ of Latter-day Saints, Salt Lake City, Utah). This was a radical thought in those days. He taught them that they were responsible for their own salvation, that they had access to every blessing the priesthood had access to, that they had equal access to the Holy Ghost and to every spiritual gift, that they also had direct access to the Savior—to model him, to become like him, to be heirs in his kingdom.

The Prophet removed some of the excuses afforded woman in her passive, dependent role and made her responsible for herself. In a very real way, he started the modern-day women's movement. Many of the early Mormon sisters caught his vision for women, got in the game, and ran with the ball. Women in Utah and Wyoming had the vote fifty years before women in the country received it generally. And as we read and ponder the writings of many nineteenth-century Latter-day Saint women, we know that they knew who they were.

Somewhere in the last eighty or so years, Mormon women have not only dropped the ball, but they have left the game. And as we have watched from the sidelines the growth of the women's movement in the hands of the world, we have been aghast at some of its excesses and some of the directions it has taken. It is the devil's pattern to imitate God's plan and to thereby deceive mankind. Whereas God wants us to know we are of equal value and importance, the devil would have us believe we are not different, but the same. The Lord's way is to become like each other only as we each take upon ourselves *all* of the Savior's traits; the devil's way would be for us to become a unisex society. We must be careful not to confuse the phony with the real thing.

Some women complain that they have no strong role models in the scriptures. That is not true, for we have many. And our main model is the same as for men—the Savior. Nowhere is it written that he is a model for men only; nowhere is it written that he came to save men only; nowhere is it written that men and women should each be allowed only half of his traits. The world has divided up character/personality traits and has labeled some of them masculine and some of them feminine. Latter-day Saints—of all people in the world—should know better than to be deceived by this. Nowhere does the Lord say that tenderness, kindness, charity, faithfulness, patience, gentleness, and compassion are female traits and should be exemplified by women only. And nowhere does he say that courage, strength, determination, leadership, and a willingness to fight—and if necessary die—for what is right should be the exclusive prerogatives of men. Any notion that God desired that women should remain passive bystanders should have been dispelled when the Prophet told women they are, from 1842 forward, responsible for their own salvation.

Not only women suffer with sexual categorization; man is also charged to become Christlike. A heavy burden is placed on him when he realizes that many of the traits that will make him Christ-like have been labeled by the world as feminine, and that by taking upon himself those characteristics he will run the risk of having his masculinity seriously questioned by his peers. In the world, in most societies throughout history, masculinity has been equated with virility or, in today's vernacular, *macho* behavior. Women have usually been considered seductive and submissive. The world, unwilling to admit the Creation, has tried to explain existence and behavior as physical and has succumbed to the process of fragmenting the whole person.

As members of the Church we find ourselves running from the present movement—which would give human beings back their wholeness—for fear of moving into a unisex society. And we are justified in running because that's the imitation. The Lord's plan is for men and women to become like each other only as we truly take upon ourselves the Savior's characteristics. If we are true to our basic natures, as the Lord has outlined them for us, our basic masculinity and femininity will not come into question. We should all possess both strength and sensitivity, courage and compassion, tenacity and tenderness. And as we best incorporate all those traits within our beings, we will be true to the male or female in us, which has been part of us since the beginning. If our sexual identity is based solely on our outward visible activities, our situation is serious indeed. The Savior was no more effeminate when he clasped the children to his bosom while in the Americas and blessed them and wept than was my great-great-grandmother unwomanly when she, as a widow, took the reins in her own hands and drove a team of oxen across the plains to Utah. If we feel that a woman lacks femininity because she is magnificent on the playing field or that a man lacks masculinity because he is a great artist, we are missing the point completely.

If the true male role is, indeed, to be obedient and sacrificial, how can a man achieve his highest potential with only macho traits? And if the woman is to reach her highest potential in her creative and nurturing role, how can she achieve it by being helpless and dependent?

President Kimball, in essence, has been urging women to get in condition, to get involved in the life around them, and to have a greater influence for good on what is happening in the world. He has urged women to become educated, to become gospel scholars, to develop every talent with which the Lord has blessed them and then to use them for the benefit of mankind. We need to learn and then teach each other the exalted role of women as revealed by the restored gospel of Jesus Christ. We need to be sure our spouses understand it. And if we have children, we need to be sure that our sons and our daughters understand it.

The Prophet Joseph said in 1842 that the key was now turned in behalf of women and that knowledge and intelligence should flow down henceforth. President Kimball put it this way to the women of the Church in September of 1979:

> Much of the major growth that is coming to the Church in the last days will come because many of the good women of the world . . . will be drawn to the Church in large numbers. This will happen to the degree that the women of the Church reflect righteousness and articulateness in their lives and to the degree that the women of the Church are seen as distinct and different—in happy ways—from the women of the world. ("The Role of Righteous Women, p. 103-4.)

And in the same talk he said:

> You must be wise in the choices that you make, but we do not desire the women of the Church to be uninformed or ineffective. You will be better mothers and wives, both in this life and in eternity, if your sharpen the skills you have been given and use the talents with which God has blessed you. (p. 103.)

We have been taught that where much is given, much is expected. If we as Latter-day Saints really understand the gospel of Jesus Christ and all it portends for women, we will realize that no blessing can be withheld from us if we are prepared and worthy to receive it. The Lord expects us to be exemplars and teachers. I pray that we may catch the understanding and vision of who we really are—and so be.

Gospel Principles
and Women

Kimberly Ford

Kimberly Ford, the chairperson of this year's fifth Annual Women's Conference, is a graduate student in Organizational Communication at Brigham Young University where she earned a B.S. degree in Family Resource Management in 1979. Kim has served as a financial representative and program coordinator for the Department of Education Weeks at BYU and has held many Church positions in service to young adults and youth. She is a capable, level-headed organizer who will contribute significantly in all that she does.

As I speak to you this morning, I speak as one who is a convert to the Mormon Church, one who has made a conscious choice to join that church. I would like first to explore some insights I have had into the Church's position on equal rights for women and then to talk about two doctrines of the Church that not only equalize Mormon women, but serve to exalt them.

The Mormon Church has often found itself out of step with the political attitudes of the day. When Joseph Smith organized the sisters of the Church in the Relief Society with this statement, "I now turn the key in your behalf in the name of the Lord, and this Society shall rejoice, and knowledge and intelligence shall flow down from this time henceforth" (Joseph Smith, *History of the Church of Jesus Christ of Latter-day Saints* [Salt Lake City: Deseret News, 1908], 4:607), women throughout this nation were oppressed by a series of unjust laws and traditions. In effect, Joseph Smith opened the door to equality not only for Latter-day Saints, but for all women.

The Mormon settlers in Utah were pioneers in more than one sense. Early in 1870, Utah women were the first in the nation to vote. Sisters made great strides in areas not previously open to women, notably in the fields of medicine and public service. In the late 1870s, Utah women began actively supporting the suffragist movement, the aim of which was to eliminate inequalities to women throughout the rest of the nation.

Not only Mormon sisters were active in seeking equality; so also were Church leaders. Women were called by the Church leaders to study medicine at eastern universities. And literary expression was encouraged, as was political involvement. President Brigham Young made this statement:

> As I have often told my sisters in the Female Relief Societies, we have sisters here who, if they had the privilege of studying, would make just as good mathematicians or accountants as any man; and we think they ought to have the privilege to study these branches of knowledge that they may develop the powers with which they are endowed. We believe that women are useful, not only to sweep houses, wash dishes, make beds, and raise babies, but that they should stand behind the counter, study law or physics, or become good bookkeepers and be able to do the business in any counting house, and all this to enlarge their sphere of usefulness for the benefit of society at large. In following these things they but answer the design of their creation. (John A. Widtsoe, comp., *Discourses of Brigham Young* [Salt Lake City: Deseret Book, 1941], pp. 216–17.)

As I have sought to understand the position of the Church with regard to women, I have heard many note with sadness that the Church's stand has changed, that the Church no longer espouses this view of women. I disagree. As I listened to the Prophet only a few months ago, I thrilled to hear these words:

> The scriptures and the prophets have taught us clearly that God, who is perfect in his attribute of justice, "is no respecter of persons" (Acts 10:24). . . . We had full equality as his spirit children. We have equality as recipients of God's perfected love for each of us. . . . We wish you to pursue and to achieve that education, therefore, which will fit you for eternity *as well as* for full service in mortality. . . . Sharpen the skills you have been given and use the talents with which God has blessed you.
>
> There is no greater and more glorious set of promises given to women than those which come through the gospel and the Church of Jesus Christ. Where else can you learn who you really are? Where else can you be given the necessary explanations and assurances about the nature of life? From what other source can you learn about your own uniqueness and identity? From whom else could you learn of our Father in Heaven's glorious plan of happiness? (Spencer W. Kimball, "The Role of Righteous Women," *Ensign,* November 1979, pp. 102–3.)

It is apparent that the regard for women as capable and intelligent beings is still being voiced by the prophet today. The doctrine remains the same.

There are times when, as a result of cultural inequities, sisters in the Church are treated unfairly. I believe President Kimball was referring to these practices when he talked to the brethren at this October's priesthood session of conference.

Sometimes we hear disturbing reports about how sisters are treated. Perhaps when this happens, it is a result of insensitivity and thoughtlessness, but it should not be, brethren. The women of this church have work to do which, though different, is equally as important as the work that we do. Their work is, in fact, the same basic work that we are asked to do—even though our roles and assignments differ. (Spencer W. Kimball, "Our Sisters in the Church," *Ensign*, November 1979, p. 49.)

The prophet teaches us that men and women are equal, that the Lord loves both the same; it is simply that their roles and assignments are different. And while men and women are *equal*, most certainly they are not the *same* as some today would have them be.

As I mentioned in my opening remarks, I wish to discuss two doctrines that differentiate Mormon women, in a positive sense, from other women. First, The Church of Jesus Christ of Latter-day Saints teaches that we are the literal spirit offspring of our Heavenly Father. Second, as such we are entitled to receive personal communication or revelation from him. As members of the Church we do not always understand completely the significance of these doctrines. Both are powerful and have a tremendous impact in terms of our human potential.

An understanding of who we are, what we are to accomplish on this earth, and our potential after this life gives us great responsibility and, surprisingly, great freedom. Stanley Milgram, a social psychologist, makes this statement about the importance of seeing the whole picture: "They did not see the larger framework of the situation, and consequently they couldn't see how to break out of it. The ability to see the larger context is precisely what we need to liberate ourselves" (Quoted by Carol Tarris in "The Frozen World of the Familiar Stranger," *Psychology Today* 8 [June 1974]:80.) The scriptures phrase it this way: "Ye shall know the truth, and the truth shall make you free" (John 8:32).

Not only does this knowledge give us freedom; the assurance that we are daughters of our Father in Heaven should also afford us a better self-concept. Imagine the impact of the idea, as Lorenzo Snow phrased it, that "as man now is, God once was; as God is, man may be." (Lorenzo Snow as quoted by Leroi C. Snow, "Devotion to Divine Inspiration," *Improvement Era*, June 1917, p. 656.) Social scientists would have a heyday determining how that belief can increase a person's self-image.

Experiences I have been through have taught me that the human being is precisely what he thinks he is. If I believe strongly enough that I can do something, and if it *is* within the realm of possibility, I can accomplish it. Since I have been a member of the Church I have come to an understanding of this principle. The knowledge that I am literally a daughter of God has changed my life.

As I discuss the second principle, personal revelation, I feel it appropriate to illustrate from my own experience.

In planning this conference, it was our desire to talk about principles, such as the equality of men and women, rather than about singular issues, such as the Equal Rights Amendment. For that reason we chose to use President Kimball's talks as the "blueprint" for our conference, feeling that it is a thorough understanding of sound principle that should determine our practices, regardless of cultural dictates. However, each person must develop his own blueprint for living. One person may need to concentrate on intellectual improvement while another ought to improve socially or spiritually. As President Kimball has the keys to receive revelation for the entire Church, so each of us has the keys to receive revelation for our own life and stewardship. We have the power within us to receive guidance directly from our Heavenly Father.

Perhaps one of the most difficult and yet rewarding things I have done has been to follow what I knew to be the promptings of the Holy Spirit and go against the desires of my parents to join this church. As dearly as I love my parents and want to please them, I had to do what I knew in my heart to be right.

Although I am fully aware of this principle of personal revelation and have experienced the powerful consequences of it in my personal life, I must admit, sadly, that I do not take full advantage of the privilege. Nor do I believe that this problem is uniquely mine. As we consider the principles we have discussed regarding the role of Latter-day Saint women, the fact that we are children of God, and the privilege of obtaining personal revelation, it is obvious that Latter-day Saints do not realize or do not take advantage of the tremendous opportunities that are theirs. Somehow we begin to take for granted the distinguishing and powerful doctrines of the Church. I cannot always defend actions of members of the Church as being just, but I will defend the principles upon which this church is built as being fair and true.

A Response,
and More Questions

Dr. Sally Barlow

Dr. Sally Barlow is currently a full-time counselor at the Brigham Young University Counseling Center. She holds a Ph.D. in Counseling Psychology from the University of Utah. She also has an MSW license. Dr. Barlow has been employed as a therapist at several mental health clinics and school districts throughout Utah. Recently she returned from Tel Aviv, where she presented a paper on group treatment for family therapy at the Third Annual International Family Therapy Conference. Dr. Barlow's comments might appropriately be entitled "A Pregnant Psychologist's Perspective" as she is presently expecting her first child.

Some time ago I began teaching a class on women's issues by asking the students (all of whom were women) to introduce themselves. The circle was completed quickly with announcements of names and majors. I then asked them to go around again and introduce themselves as their best friends might, hoping to encourage a broader range of feelings and roles. I also suggested that some of them might be in the class because, for whatever reason, they were experiencing some pain from being a woman in today's world. Later—as we compared the two types of introductions and talked about conflicts, questions, and struggles—a woman turned to me and said, "What do you mean by 'pain from being a woman'? Do you mean physical or mental? I don't understand." Her question was sincere, her face genuinely puzzled. She went on to describe her life and her love of the gospel, her husband, and their soon-to-come baby. Several other women looked equally curious. A lively discussion followed between the *pained* and the *unpained*.

I left the class wondering, once again, why some people are happier than others. I had taught a similar class at another university where pain, anger, and discrimination were immediately agreed upon as common experiences among women. Were BYU students really any different? Were they just denying their frustrations, or were they living better lives? Was it true for all of them or just a small minority? Were they young and inexperienced, untouched by the real world, or were their lives qualitatively different? I didn't know the answers then, and I still don't. I hesitate to compare small segments of society—that makes for spurious generalizations. But it did raise all sorts of questions that have forced me to address the issue: Does living the gospel's precepts help people avoid pain? Is a pain-free existence a promised result of a righteous life?

I learned long ago that stock answers are as confining as stock questions. A wise little girl once said, "Please, God, help me to ask the real questions. If you ask the question in two dimensions you get the answer in two dimensions. It's like a box. You can't get out." (Fynn, *Mr. God, This is Anna* [New York: Holt, Rinehart and Winston, 1974].)

In an attempt to take the lid off, I asked myself these questions: where is the fine line between necessary pain and unnecessary pain; and how does the difference between principle and practice contribute to such pain?

It is immensely important to acknowledge both over the pulpit and in the privacy of our hearts that struggle is not necessarily synonymous with sin. All through the ages we have known this from the writings of prophets, philosophers, lay people, and the like. Life is difficult. That's that. No one gets through it unscathed. Nevertheless, as we get bumped and bruised we need to ask ourselves, "Am I involved in self-exploration or self-indulgence?" I have worked as a psychologist in several different settings and have seen both kinds of clients. I've asked myself, "Is this person (or am I) going over old territory, retelling stories again and again (e.g., bad upbringing, insensitive bishops, automobile wrecks)—abusing problems of environment and circumstance to account for problems of personality or character?"

This is not to say that environment does not contribute to personality ills. It does. We've all heard of, or have had done to us, acts ranging from the harmful to the unimaginable. But we can only shackle ourselves to the fates and the furies for just so long before they become our excuse for failing. As Goethe suggested, we eventually assume the mask if we wear it long enough. How awful to be imprisoned in our own biology or circumstance. The hope of rising above heredity and environment is the only thing that separates us from the lower species.

We must understand the unfairnesses of life. That is what listening neighbors, professionals, or loving friends are for. But then we have to move on. We can usually tell the difference between complete indulgence in pain and complete denial of it. Neither position is healthy. It is detecting the difference between subtle martyrdom and stoicism that is difficult for us and others to do. And it is at this juncture that we may be less able to move on because we haven't yet acknowledged where we are.

That brings me to the issue of depression. Why is it such a hot topic these days? Is it simply the product of a media event, the reflection of societal pressures, or sincere personal pain turned chronic and experienced by enough people (particularly women) that it has become a national phenomenon? I suppose it is a combination of all those factors and many others. Once again, I don't know what the answer is, but I do know that we should be asking ourselves some questions.

There is a point at which acute mental pain becomes chronic. Mental health professionals would label that *depression.* Depression is the immobilization of feelings—anger, jealously, hurt, disappointment—all the negative ones. Unfortunately, when we numb ourselves to those we also become numb to joy, love, excitement, and other positive feelings. It involves a complicated chemical process mediated by what neurophysiologists label the "limbic system" and several very important elements called "neurotransmitters." When we are afraid to have real pain—pain caused by events such as, losses, deaths, and inner struggles—we convert it into the immobilizing blanket of depression. If it goes on long enough it actually affects us physically by interfering with the thought and feeling processes mediated in the brain and central nervous system. A vicious cycle begins in that the psyche affects the body and then the body affects the psyche. The end result may be a debilitating depression or even suicide. Being able to say, "I hurt" or "I'm angry" allows us to have the feeling and not hide it on the one hand or wallow in it on the other.

We've all heard horror stories about a bishop or Relief Society president, for example, making doctrinally unfounded and hence potentially harmful statements. It is easy to see how such mistakes contribute to a person's pain. I believe women are hurt more often than men by such remarks for one reason: research has shown that women grow up dependent on others for their self-esteem (See "Depression and Learned Helplessness," in R. J. Friedman and M. M. Katz, eds., *The Psychology of Depression: Contemporary Theory and Research* [San Francisco: W. H. Freedman Press, 1975], pp. 219–21). They are more likely to believe what they hear. For example, they respond to the myth of Super Mom or Super Single Sister, and they seldom stop to think whether or not it is reasonable for them to live that way.

Actually, in such situations we should be glad for the pain. It slows us down, hopefully to the point of being introspective and examining the expectations with which we enshroud ourselves. We can't go blithely on after hearing a person in authority say something like, "Elders, use your priesthood. Otherwise you might as well be women." Whatever the person's intent, there is an implicit message: Women, you are less than men. Not just different—but less. And that hurts. So what are we going to do about it? Leave the Church?

From 1950 to 1970 some interesting research was conducted on what was called the phenomenon of convergence (See H. S. Pepinsky, "Convergence: A Phenomenon in Counseling," in *American Psychologist,* 19(1964):373–8). What it said, essentially, was that people gave up what their five senses told them to be true in the face of contradictory opinions, even though unbeknownst to them, people in the experiment were paid to contradict the first person's opinion no matter what was really true. We are often afraid to stand by what we see, hear, taste, smell, or touch. We have to cultivate our own values carefully by testing them, by standing up for them.

In addition, there is some exciting preliminary research that indicates possible differences between female and male brain functions that may give us more definitive answers about a woman's intuition. This intuition, or immediate knowing seemingly based on no concrete evidence, may be a right hemisphere product more prominent in women, a real phenomenon and not mere poppycock. So for whatever reason, whether it's what our five senses tell us or what our intuition tells us, we need to learn to trust ourselves. Most importantly, if we're not sure about our senses or our intuition, we can use our most powerful tool, personal revelation.

Once again, we must walk a very fine line. If we relied solely on expert opinion, what we believed about ourselves and the world would simply be a matter of which expert we happened to believe. For example, Milton believed women to be the "fairest of creation! last and best of all God's works!" (F. S. Mead, *Encyclopedia of Religious Quotations* [New Jersey: Fleming Revell Co., 1965], p. 471). On the other hand, Samuel Johnson once said, "A woman preaching is like a dog's walking on his hind legs. It is not done well; but you are surprised to find it done at all" (*Ibid,* p. 470). We can find equally divergent opinions in modern-day Mormondom on the subject of women or, for that matter, on many other issues. The question is, "How can we make subtle distinctions within the recesses of our soul without clinging to an external, polarized resource?"

The issue then is the fine line between commonsense self-reliance and dangerous self-reliance. Commonsense self-reliance is, for example, using our five senses to give us information about the world. It is being able to stand by our feelings, beliefs, and experiences even though someone else might say, "You're crazy." However, complete self-reliance can be a dangerous thing. C. S. Lewis said, "The first principle of Hell is, I am my own" (C. S. Lewis, *Mere Christianity* [New York: MacMillan Co., 1952], p. 108). G. K. Chesterton added, "Complete self reliance is not merely a sin, (it) is a weakness. Believing utterly in oneself is a hysterical and superstitious belief." (G. K. Chesterton, *Orthodoxy* [Massachusetts: Plimpton Press, 1908], p. 23.) As Latter-day Saints, we believe that God ultimately has the last say. And it is here where reliance on an outside authority is sound. On the issue of other authorities, the Lord gave us good advice— test it out in your heart, try it on, see if it fits. But when it comes to his advice, it is clear how he means for us to use it, and what the rewards will be if we do so: "For whosoever shall do the will of my Father which is in heaven, the same is my brother, and sister, and mother" (Matthew 12:50).

The answers that are easily obtained are the ones having to do with clearly opposite viewpoints. And often these answers aren't worth having. They make us take a rigid stand, close our eyes and ears, and refuse to deal with the more subtle and frightening issues of life. All the answers that are worth struggling for are the fine-line ones, the ones between necessary pain and unnecessary pain, between principle and practice. Rather than creating a box around us, a six-sided prison, such honest struggling surrounds us with a prism—a multitude of possibilities that fashion for us, from every angle, the immense challenge God gave us: to be perfect. That is an incredible hope. But it isn't a gift; it must be purchased at a great price. And the constant balancing of fine lines is solely for the sharpening of our countenances, our personalities, so that we will be ready for him.

The Traditional Role
of the Mormon Woman

Colleen Maxwell

Colleen Maxwell has held many positions of responsibility in the Church, including Primary president, MIA president, Relief Society president, and member of the General Board of the Young Women's MIA. She holds a bachelor's degree in home economics from the University of Utah. Sister Maxwell is married to Elder Neal A. Maxwell, one of the seven Presidents of the First Quorum of the Seventy. Elder Maxwell describes his wife as one who "doesn't care for status but prefers to be in the trenches of the neighborhood, meeting the silent needs of those around her."

I am appreciative of the opportunity to contemplate my attitudes and feelings regarding my experience in the so-called *intact* or *traditional* family. And while I speak from my perspective, this does not mean that I have any less respect and admiration for those in other circumstances.

Having come from a different time and age, with different attitudes and fewer choices, I realize that some things that are questioned by some today were *givens* in my day. However, the longer I live, the more grateful I am for the gift of those givens. These are difficult and complex days for young women. Fortunately, most young Latter-day Saint women today are equal to the challenge.

I recognize that society is dependent on the services and help that is given by so many capable women, and I appreciate that I could not fulfill my role completely without these services.

Our family is one with a highly involved and very busy husband and father who has a great commitment to the gospel, to family, and to his work. It includes four children, all of whom are married; five grandchildren, who are the light of our lives; and me, the wife, mother, grandmother, homemaker, and servant of my Heavenly Father, and a former school teacher.

Though I hesitate speaking personally, I assume the expectation is that I will express some of my feelings about my role in this family. The fact that I grew up wanting and looking forward to the traditional role of home-maker and mother has no doubt helped to make it very acceptable and satisfying to me. I have not been the least disappointed.

I frankly appreciated the fact that my husband agreed with me in want-ing to remain basically a homemaker and that I could be allowed to do just that. Outside activities and ceremonial chores came gradually, but they did come, and sometimes they have been demanding enough to cause a little resentment. Although, having said that, I recognize the expectations of other have helped me to grow.

There seems to have been an unspoken arrangement in our marriage in that my husband's involvements and my own took turns. I was a Primary president. Then he was a bishop. Next I became a Relief Society president. And so on. (Of course, his present calling indirectly involves me a great deal.) This arrangement made it more possible for each of us to be helpful and supportive of the other. And certainly these experiences enriched the whole family.

Perhaps I should be reluctant to acknowledge that through the success and recognition that has come to my husband, there has been sufficient to carry me. I actually haven't felt much additional need for recognition. That feeling may not hold true for everyone.

I don't deny there have been a few bad days over the years when I played the *martyr mother* role and have experienced *cabin fever*. But the key for me has been having an understanding and very appreciative husband. Further, whenever I felt like complaining or grumbling very loudly, I would catch myself and count my blessings. My husband and I have worked hard at parenting, but it is work that has usually been fun. We have quite a few specific little things we do to enrich our traditional home because in family life, the little things are often the big things.

I have been grateful for demands of Church and family because it is easy to see how one could otherwise get caught up in self-pity and self-concern. I quite agree with someone who said, "Hell is being frozen in self-pity."

The understanding I have of the gospel of Jesus Christ and of my role in it has given me purpose. The example of his life and, in particular, that he "came not to be ministered unto, but to minister" (Mark 10:45) has been my philosophy and ultimate joy. He also said, "For their sakes [do] I sanctify myself" (John 17:19). This posture is not always easy to maintain, but it is *always* the most gratifying.

Pat Boone's wife made a profound statement on a talk show once when she said she began to ask herself, when she and her husband were having some differences, why she seemed to love her children so completely. Then she realized it was because she didn't have certain expectations in her love for them. And when she came to have that same unconditional love for her husband, she was much happier.

I learned another lesson from a wise friend who, although she is not a member of the Church, gave me a good insight. Her husband had sustained several injuries necessitating her giving up all her civic and social activities (which were many) for a year to be with him. She said it was one of the best years they had had together. She maintained that sacrifice is good for a marriage and added that sometimes Mormon women feel too secure within the concept of celestial marriage and as a result, ironically, don't give as much as they should to the relationship. The husband-wife relationship is the prime relationship and should have prime time. If lights go out in that relationship, there won't be much light in any other relationships.

The thing that has been most challenging to me is to be less *task-oriented* and to be more *people-oriented*. I would like to have felt that the *Mary* in me came to the fore a bit more often. I recognize that someone like Martha must attend to getting the supper on the table, but I also feel that conversing and listening are an important balance. These are hard choices—bound to be frustrating—but then again, we were never told it would be easy.

One cannot deny that it is great to be one's own boss—unless the taskmaster is too demanding. It seems most people make the assumption that at the beginning of each day we have twenty-four hours to dispose of just as we choose. We may resent the demands made of our time that are not of our choosing. However, each hour and day is God-given, and, as King Benjamin commented in Mosiah 2:21, "God preserves us by lending us breath." Coming to fully accept that notion should assist us all to be less self-serving.

Although the traditional wife and homemaker role has been the one I have chosen and have been privileged to pursue, the basic response of all Mormon women to the world should be the same for each—whatever the circumstance—to be "in the world but not of it" and to keep the Lord's commandments in a world filled with tribulation. We should never lose sight of that strategy even though there may be tactical differences in our circumstances.

The tactical pressures do differ. For instance, the LDS single woman competing in the professional world may have somewhat different temptations and enticements then the LDS middle-aged homemaker (meaning me), but we must both keep the seventh commandment.

On the other hand, the LDS homemaker may have, in addition, anxieties and concerns about rearing her children in a permissive society.

The single woman who is dating may have to worry about her own behavior on dates, whereas the married woman of teenage children worries about several individuals who are dating.

Clearly there isn't one set of Ten Commandments for the married woman and another for the single, divorced, or widowed.

Regardless of circumstance, we all should stay close to the scriptures. Finding the time to do that adequately may be more of a challenge for a busy young mother than for the older or the single woman.

The single woman may have to deal with more loneliness because, frankly, even with Christian service, Church service, and social activities, the single woman could still have some lonely hours. And again, loneliness can deteriorate into self-pity if she's not careful.

I am grateful that I am a woman because in our society it seems women find it easier to follow the Lord's admonition to lose our lives in the service of others. Personally, service provides a great deal of satisfaction even though attempted meagerly. Elder Bruce R. McConkie wisely said, "It isn't sufficient to keep the commandments—we must also serve our fellowmen" (Statement made at Mission Presidents' Seminar, Edinburgh, Scotland, August 1978).

Everyone's sample of humanity varies. We may wish for a different sample to work with, but what we do with our sample is an indication of our spirituality. In Alma 29:3 we read: "For I ought to be content with the things which the Lord hath allotted unto me." We should not be in rebellion over our opportunities, because these may contain the very experiences we need most.

The need for strong, sweet families is greater than ever because much of the reinforcement the family once received from society is being stripped away.

To quote from Brigitte Berger's article on "What Women Want," she says modernity opened up a hitherto unimagined range of options, yet their very number has resulted in more confusion than happiness.

She also states, "American women are giving up on the family and the private sphere at the very moment in history when it is coming to be argued with increasing frequency that work (per se) can no longer endow life with a sense of meaning."

Even for me in the home, as I grow older, the things of most import (and where I find greater satisfaction) are the relationships. I jealously try to guard some of my time to enjoy those relationships without neglecting the Christian service President Kimball has urged upon us, both by his words and his deeds.

A woman who doesn't undertand her true identity and the purpose of life can never really be liberated. Until she overcomes that ignorance, happiness will be an illusion.

The keeping of the commandments brings fulfillment. Trying to find fulfillment other ways will be an empty exercise.

I am so grateful for the gospel of Jesus Christ, which helps me see these things with greater clarity.

Talents

Yoshie Akimoto Eldredge

Yoshie Akimoto Eldredge is an accomplished concert pianist. Since studying music at the Juilliard School of Music in New York for six years with the eminent James Friskin and Sasha Gorodnitski, Sister Eldredge has performed as a guest soloist for numerous festivals and civic organizations throughout the United States and Japan, and she currently performs regularly in the Community Concert Series sponsored by Columbia Artists Management. Currently Sister Eldredge serves as director of the Akimoto Piano Studio. She is married to Stephen Eldredge who has served as a bishop and in the stake presidency of the Los Angeles Stake. They have three children.

Prior to Yoshie's remarks it might be interesting to review a segment of the comments from the Phil Donahue show 12 December 1979:

Donahue: The main purpose for women being here is to raise and nurture children?
Caller: No, not necessarily. A woman can raise her family in the home and nurture her husband and still have interests and do things.
Donahue: Can she have a job?
Caller: Like I said, only if it was absolutely necessary. That's the way I feel.
Donahue: What if she's extraordinarily talented? What if she's Madame Curie?
Caller: No, because you're getting away from your home. I think that you have things within your home, arts and things that you can do.
Donahue: Right. Suppose that you were a brilliant concert pianist.
Caller   You can still be at home and do that.
Donahue: But you can't go out onto Carnegie Hall and go on the road.
Sonia Johnson: Do you think God made a mistake when he gave women those talents? They surely are wasted if you are a brilliant concert pianist and you can't perform. Why do we have those talents, then?
(*Phil Donahue Show,* December 12, 1979, Chicago, Illinois: A transcript released by the producers of the show, p. 15.)

Abraham Lincoln once stated, "All I am or ever hope to be, I owe to my angel mother." In many respects, I would like to echo his words. My angel mother was an outstanding musician. As she discovered musical talent in her daughters, she determined we would also be musicians and, specifically, pianists.

From my earliest years, under the direction of my mother, I prepared to become a concert pianist. In numerous interviews in my teens I was asked what my ambitions were, and to these questions I always responded that I wanted to become a great concert pianist. I also recall adding to that ambition the desire to become a mother. As I reflect upon this added objective, it stands out to me as a reflection of woman's natural desire planted in her by her Maker.

By the time I reached my early twenties, I had established myself as a successful concert pianist in Japan and had begun to build a foundation for the same in the United States. I had also become an active member of The Church of Jesus Christ of Latter-day Saints and had adopted values and standards that I knew were critical for my personal growth and happiness. For a Latter-day Saint who is a concert soloist, whether an instrumentalist or a vocalist, there are basic questions and choices that must be dealt with early in one's career. Marriage, by worldly standards and by the standards of some of my good friends who are regularly performing on the concert stage around the globe, is not something for which one sacrifices one's career. The thought of rearing children is also unacceptable for those women pursuing such a career. Yet despite the standards of the world among my peers at the Juilliard School and on concert tours, I knew that marriage and motherhood were two of the most important goals in my life and that to be successful in both, sacrifices would have to be made and selflessness exhibited each day.

Now, years later, I look back on decisions I have made along the way, and I am deeply grateful for the teachings of the Church and for my husband and children who have filled my life with joy and satisfaction. I am also grateful to my husband for his support of my career. We have found in our marriage that no division of work in the home need exist. Instead, each partner strives to fill in the gaps and do what is required, regardless of who did it last or whose duty it traditionally has been. Teamwork in marriage can facilitate the development of a marvelous relationship that allows for the success of both partners. The primary requisite for both the husband and the wife is selflessness. More than any other factor, selflessness facilitates realization of the goal that was ordained of God when he said, referring to all couples married under the authority of God, "They shall be one flesh" (Genesis 2:24).

My husband and I made a decision early in our marriage that I would continue to give concerts as often as possible, even though such a course might be difficult for all concerned. We planned to limit the concerts while the children were young and to increase them as the children grew older and eventually had families of their own. We have since been on enough concert road trips to know we do not want a concert career that entails sixty to one hundred concerts each year around the world. Our objective will be perhaps ten to fifteen concerts per year within the United States, with an occasional return to my homeland for a concert tour.

In recent years, our family has grown in size (three children, ages nine, three, and nine months), and the number of concerts has been reduced to only a few a year. In addition to duties at work and home, my husband was called to serve as a bishop for two and one-half years and as a counselor in a stake presidency for two years, at which time we moved to a new area. He also served as a volunteer for the Boy Scouts of America. All these duties meant he was away from home much of the time. During this time I served as ward Primary president, teacher, choir director, organist, and in other Church positions. I also taught ten or more piano students each week. I found I would go for months without practicing the piano. When a concert invitation would come, often on short notice, I would frantically prepare with much trepidation. Such irregular involvement in music caused me to wonder at times why I had been given the gift of music if I was not to utilize it. I also wondered if the time would come again when I would return to full activity as a pianist.

In the process of this heavy Church involvement, I discovered the true meaning of serving the youth and the elderly, caring for the sick, sacrificing myself for my children, and generally looking beyond myself and seeing the needs of others. I have adopted values and priorities that allow me to place in perspective those choices that I must make in my life. These priorities, in order of importance, are: first, to come to know God the Father and his Son, Jesus Christ, intimately and personally and to learn to obey the will of God; second, to be a loyal and faithful wife to my husband and to do all I can to ensure a happy marriage; third, to be an effective and devoted mother to the children in our home; fourth, to be a laborer in Zion; and fifth, to develop my talents and abilities, including the pursuit of a career as a concert pianist.

Clearly, if my sole objective in life were to become a world-touring concert pianist, my goals would be different than noted (though I am giving more concerts at this time than I have for several years). While I might be criticized for placing the development of God-given talents and gifts fifth on the list, in view of my convictions and experience I know this is right. My devotion to my children as their mother takes precedence over the development of my own talent. My responsibility as the mother in the home is to ensure that my children come to an early understanding of who they are and the purposes of life and have opportunity to learn as much as I can give them prior to their graduation from the university of the home. I am also determined to provide for each child musical training and other opportunities to develop their skills so that their lives will be blessed with music and with the discipline and work habits associated with musical training. Our children will be mothers, fathers, and leaders of the future, and my firm determination is to prepare those under my charge to succeed.

118

Notwithstanding these higher priorities and responsibilities outside the field of music, I feel I am progressing as a musician. I recall the words of a music critic in Japan who reviewed one of my concerts in my early teens and commented that, "This outstanding young pianist performed the work beautifully, but now needs to experience life and its trauma in depth that the interpretations and depth of understanding projected in the performance will be more equal to the majesty of the composition."

I have learned to appreciate those words of wisdom. Indeed, I feel I have grown immensely as a person and as a musician since those early years, in no small part because of the challenges and trials experienced in my complex life, in which I have tried to make every effort to succeed as a wife, mother, and pianist. As to the trauma noted by the critic, there has been abundant trauma in my life—to the point where I have, at times, felt I could not continue. But then proddings would come, and after much prayer and inner struggle, I have known it was right to continue striving. While I feel the Lord has allowed tribulations and vicissitudes to occur in my life to expand my soul, I feel he will yet allow me time and opportunity to prepare and display my ability to its fullest to suit his purposes in building his kingdom. In moments of desperation, when I have leaned on him the most, my Heavenly Father has been there to support and to manifest his perfect love for one of his daughters.

Because of all the experiences of my life, my understanding of music and my ability to express it have grown greatly. The expressions of composers, in different moods and colors, come to me as a reality of life, as if such expressions were my own. I become involved in the music more intensely than ever before. The music causes me to weep in its sorrow, exult in its joy, suffer with its desire unfulfilled, dance in its beauty, grieve in its tragedy, weep for its fulfillment of faith and love of God.

There are some developments and growth that take place within us that cannot be rushed, that occur only commensurate with the experiences in life, and that cause us to stretch and struggle and overcome. I am reminded that Joseph Smith, Jr., and other great leaders in history were given tremendous responsibilities to accomplish and yet faced opposition, perilous tribulations, and afflictions throughout their lives. Thus, if it is difficult for me to pursue the development of my talents in my given circumstances, I need but look to the examples of others for inspiration to reach upward. Attaining lofty goals is never easy.

My motivation for the development of my talent is not to gain satisfaction in receiving worldly fame and glory or to compete with others. I always have felt very strongly from my youth that the gift or talent that the Lord placed in me belongs to the Lord. It is not mine. He has loaned it to me, and I am responsible to develop it for his special purpose. I must develop it to the highest level in my power, and I must share its beauty with others around me.

To become a great musician, mother, leader, or a great person in any field, I feel, one must work to build all the major facets of one's life. It is similar to planning and constructing a house. If the architect becomes engrossed in the size and beauty of one upstairs room and neglects another room on the ground floor, the entire structure may not only appear distorted, but it may even collapse. This is so even though the upstairs room may be truly magnificent by itself. The ground floor of the individual, his or her character and integrity, requires continual attention and improvement so that the whole person remains balanced and intact and the special talents and abilities can be properly nurtured and magnified.

To become successful as a human being, one needs to experience the realities of life and develop the capacity to serve others and the strength to rise above the trials placed before him. The happiness and joy of womanhood in my life is a witness to me that my course is right for me, and for that witness I thank my Father in Heaven each day.

Whenever I play, it is my humble expression and testimony, my love and appreciation to the Lord. I am grateful for the stewardship of this gift.

Women in the
Light of the Gospel

Carolyn J. Rasmus

Carolyn J. Rasmus was recently appointed Administrative Assistant to the President of Brigham Young University. She holds a doctorate in Physical Education, with a minor in Child Development and Learning Disabilities. She has published numerous articles dealing with health, physical education, and recreation. Sister Rasmus serves as chairman of the Faculty Advisory Council and also the Committee on Women's Concerns. She is the beloved stake Young Women's president of the Provo, Utah, Edgemont Stake.

This past October I attended the Women's Conference at the University of Utah. One of the sessions was entitled "Mormon Women: Three Perspectives." I listened with interest to the panel members and the three women who responded. I have reflected frequently on the ideas and concerns expressed at that session. In retrospect I have found it interesting that there were few if any references to the scriptures, teachings of the Church, or words of our prophets. My perspective, as a Mormon woman, was not expressed in that session, and I am grateful for this opportunity to share my viewpoints and beliefs.

I want to preface my comments with some personal background for those of you not acquainted with me. I came to Brigham Young University ten years ago this past fall to begin work on a graduate degree. I selected BYU because I had become professionally acquainted with one of the faculty members here, and I wanted to study with her. I knew little about BYU and less about Mormons. Yet when I came to this campus, I felt at home; I was comfortable here. I sensed the difference that is frequently spoken of by visitors to our campus. I had come here on a one-year leave of absence from Iowa State University, but when it came time to return to my position, I resigned so that I could stay and complete my studies. The following summer, a class of students whom I had taught presented me with a triple combination. That gift, and the sincerity and

121

feeling with which it was presented, had a great impact on my life. I began a serious investigation of the Church, its teachings, and beliefs. In March 1971 I became a member of The Church of Jesus Christ of Latter-day Saints. I joined the Church after much study and against the wishes of my parents and protests of my friends. I joined the Church because I believed that the Prophet Joseph Smith had indeed received a revelation from our Heavenly Father to restore the gospel in these latter days.

As I have continued to study the scriptures and explore the teachings of the Church, my testimony of it has been strengthened. I have found new and expanded understandings, as well as meaningful purpose and direction to my life as a woman and particularly as a Latter-day Saint woman.

Since my conversion, I have often wished that I had been raised in a Latter-day Saint home and that my parents and other members of my family had a testimony of the restored gospel. However, I am becoming increasingly grateful that I have been recently converted, for I find that I am able to separate the teachings of the Church from those cultural practices that frequently are accepted as being doctrinal. It is the *teachings* of the Church I will discuss today.

We live in a time when there is much talk about equality and equal rights. The scriptures and the prophets have clearly taught that "God is no respecter of persons" (Acts 10:34). President Kimball reaffirmed this when he spoke to the women of the Church this past fall. He said, "We had full equality as his spirit children. We have equality as recipients of God's perfected love for each of us." (Spencer W. Kimball, "The Role of Righteous Women," *Ensign,* November 1979, p. 102.)

Equality, however, does *not* imply sameness. Although men and women are equal in the sight of the Lord, their eternal roles and assignments differ. Men's primary duties are associated with fatherhood and the priesthood; women have stewardship responsibilities in the areas of motherhood and sisterhood. By virtue of these assignments, men are directly responsible for Church governance; their duties are organizational and administrative. Women, on the other hand, have the assigned responsibility to create and nurture.

Because men are holders of the priesthood, and therefore often more visible in the operations of the Church, some people assume men are more important and competent than women. John A. Widtsoe made clear that the priesthood is not a reward for competency or excellence:

> Women of a congregation . . . may be wise, far greater in mental powers, even greater in actual power of leadership than men who preside over them. That signifies nothing. The priesthood is . . . given to good men and they exercise it by right of divine gift, called upon by the leaders of the Church. (*Priesthood and Church Government* [Salt Lake City: Deseret Book Co., 1939], p. 90.)

On another occasion he said, "No man who understands the gospel believes that he is greater than his wife, or more beloved of the Lord, because he holds the priesthood" (*Evidences and Reconciliations* [Salt Lake City: Bookcraft, 1960], pp. 307-8).

Although women do not hold the priesthood, they are partakers of every blessing and privilege of the priesthood. Nowhere is this clearer than in the temple endowment. The ordinances of the temple are all priesthood in nature, but women have access to all of them. The instructions, ordinances, and convenants that are part of the temple endowment are the same for men and women. It is in the temple that men are prepared for their roles as kings and priests. Likewise, women are prepared to become queens and priestesses. Woman stands beside the man, "a joint inheritor with him in the fullness of all things. Exaltation and eternal increase is her part as well as his. Godhood is not for men only; it is for men and women together." (Bruce R. McConkie, *Mormon Doctrine* [Salt Lake City: Bookcraft, 1966], p. 844.)

The differences between men and women are designed to be complementary and unifying, not divisive and separating. The ultimate plan is for the achievement of a perfect balance, with neither sex to be unduly emphasized. President Kimball reinforced this concept when he spoke of marriage as a full partnership. "We do not want our LDS women to be silent partners or limited partners in that eternal assignment. Please," he said to women, "be a contributing and full partner." (Spencer W. Kimball, "Privileges & Responsibilities of Sisters," *Ensign,* November 1978, p. 106.)

In addition to recognizing the differences between the eternal roles and assignments of men and those of women, we must be aware that women do have qualities and characteristics that distinguish them from men—and vice versa. Elder Bruce R. McConkie emphasized and paid tribute to some of these feminine equalities during his remarks at the dedication of the Nauvoo Monument to Women. He suggested that if we consider Adam and Eve as prototypes of ourselves, male and female, then the nature of their complementary relationship can be instructive. Adam desired to obey God's commandment against partaking of the forbidden fruit; his choice was to strictly obey the law. Eve, on the other hand, possessed a more intuitive understanding of their purpose for being. She recognized that in order for the human race to come about, she and Adam simply had no choice but to partake of the fruit. She was, in this instance, keenly sensitive to the existence of a higher law.

Rebecca provides another example of a woman's spiritual insight. Elder McConkie went on to suggest that she understood her obligation to "engineer and . . . arrange so that things are done in a way that will result in the salvation of more of our Father's children" ("Our Sisters from the Beginning," *Ensign,* January 1979, p. 63). You will remember that Isaac, Rebecca's aged husband, was preparing, in accordance with the law, to pronounce a special blessing upon his firstborn son, Esau. Rebecca knew, however, that it was their righteous son Jacob, not Esau, who should have the blessing, for the Lord had revealed it to her before the children were born. Therefore, she engineered the situation so that her husband did indeed confer the blessings of Abraham upon Jacob. Here we have another demonstration of obedience to higher law.

Elder McConkie is quick to affirm that women have, from the beginning, been entitled to impressive spiritual endowments. He indicates that

> Where spiritual things are concerned, as pertaining to all the gifts of
> the spirit, with reference to receiving revelation, the gaining of
> testimonies, the seeing of visions, in all matters that pertain to
> Godliness and holiness and which are brought to pass as a result of
> personal righteousness—in all these things men and women stand in a
> position of absolute equality before the Lord. ("Our Sisters from the
> Beginning," p. 61.)

The differences between men and women are eternal differences. Not only are men and women gifted differently to accomplish the purpose of providing mortal bodies for immortal spirits, but they have differing qualities and strengths, as well as unique ways of perceiving the same experiences. The whole truth emerges only when both perceptions are applied. Acknowledgment of these differences lends special significance to the apostle Paul's observation that "neither is the man without the woman, neither the woman without the man, in the Lord" (1 Corinthians 11:11).

I agree totally with the concluding paragraph of a paper prepared last year by the Advisory Committee on Women's Concerns at BYU. It reads as follows:

> As we come to realize how essential this two-sided vision is in the
> search for and assimilation of truth, in the daily living of lives, in the
> happy functioning of families, we are impressed to suggest that
> women should be asked to bring their unique perspective to decision-
> making councils and committees in both the University and the
> Church. Just as women need the support and counsel of men in their
> particular Church callings, so do men need the support and counsel
> of women in theirs. If women in the Church were indeed valued and
> counseled with in this reciprocal manner, "Women's Issues" as we
> know them would be largely resolved. ("Thoughts on the Concerns of
> Mormon Women at Brigham Young University and Elsewhere," 29 May
> 1979, p. 12.)

While I am convinced that full equality of men and woman is an important precept of the restored gospel, I also realize that too often there is a disparity between our doctrines and our actual practices. The prophet himself acknowledged this when he spoke to men of the Church in the priesthood session of general conference last October. After describing specific ways in which sisters of the Church were being treated condescendingly, President Kimball made an all-important distinction: "I mention all these things, my brethren, not because the doctrine or the teachings of the Church are in doubt, but because in some situations our behavior is of doubtful quality" ("The Role of Righteous Women," p. 49).

President Kimball has counseled us as women of the Church to appreciate the gospel's implications concerning the eternal nature of our individual identities and the uniqueness of our personalities. He has stressed the importance of experiencing for ourselves the perfect love our Father in Heaven has for each of us and of knowing the value that he places upon us as individuals. There is no question that our prophet expects women to reach their highest potential—eternal progression and the possibility of Godhood. I believe that his admonition to the women of the Church is to help prepare us for our immensely important role in building up the latter-day kingdom. You will recall his encouragement to study the scriptures, set goals, apply ourselves, and learn all we can. Remember, he said that women should be as concerned about their capacity to communicate as they are about their ability to sew and preserve food. We are encouraged to develop our talents and to seek excellence in every righteous endeavor. President Kimball has prophesied that our gifts and spiritual strengths will be desperately needed prior to the second coming of our Savior. The righteous woman's strength and influence, he reminds us, can today be ten-fold what it might have been in more tranquil times.

He has also told us—

> Much of the major growth that is coming to the Church in the last days will come because many of the good women of the world (in whom there is often such an inner sense of spirituality) will be drawn to the Church in large numbers. This will happen to the degree that the women of the Church reflect righteousness and articulateness in their lives and to the degree that women of the Church are seen as distinct and different—in happy ways—from the women of the world. Thus it will be that the female examplars of the Church will be a significant force in both the numerical and the spiritual growth of the Church in these last days. ("The Role of Righteous Women," pp. 103-4.)

I have found that the scriptures and teachings of the Church have helped me to better understand my place in the eternal scheme of things. As a result of my conversion, I have become personally acquainted with the Savior and his saving principles. I have experienced in my life direction, vision, and that peace "which passeth all understanding." I strive daily to overcome weaknesses and to prepare myself to participate in building up the kingdom of God in preparation for the second coming of our Savior.